TEACHER'S PET PUBLICATIONS

PUZZLE PACK
for
Beowulf
based on classic epic work by
Anonymous

Written by
William T. Collins

© 2005 Teacher's Pet Publications
All Rights Reserved

The materials in this packet are copyrighted
by Teacher's Pet Publications, Inc.

These pages may be duplicated by the purchaser
for use in the purchaser's own classroom.

Copying any of these materials and distributing them
for any other purpose is a violation of the copyright laws.

© 2005 Teacher's Pet Publications, Inc.
www.tpet.com

INTRODUCTION
If you already own the LitPlan for this title, this Puzzle Pack will refresh your Unit Resource Materials and Vocabulary Resource Materials sections plus give you additional materials you can substitute into the tests. If you do not already have a complete LitPlan, these pages will give you some supplemental materials to use with your own plan. There are two main groups of materials: one set for unit words (such as characters' names, symbols, places, etc.) and one set for vocabulary words associated with the book.

WORD LIST
There is a word list for both the unit words and the vocabulary words. These lists show you which words are being used in the materials and the clues or definitions being used for those words. You may want to give students a word list with clues/definitions to help them, or you may want students to only have a word list (without clues/definitions) if you want them to work a little harder. Both are available for duplication. The word lists can also be your "calling key" for the bingo games.

FILL IN THE BLANK AND MATCHING
There are 4 each of the fill in the blank and matching worksheets for both the unit and vocabulary words. These pages can be used either as extra worksheets for students or as objective parts of a unit test. They can be done individually if students need extra help or as a whole class activity to review the material covered.

MAGIC SQUARES
The magic squares not only reinforce the material covered but also work on reasoning and math skills. Many teachers have told us that their students really enjoy doing these!

WORD SEARCH PUZZLES
The word search words go in all directions, as indicated on your answer keys. Two of the word search puzzles have the clues listed rather than the words. This makes the puzzle a little more difficult, but it reinforces the material better. Two word search puzzles have words only for students who find the clue puzzles too difficult.

CROSSWORD PUZZLES
Both unit and vocabulary word sections have 4 crossword puzzles.

BINGO CARDS
There are 32 individual bingo cards for the unit words and 32 individual bingo cards for the vocabulary words. You can use your word list as a "call list," calling the words at random and marking them off of your list as you go, or you could use the flash cards by cutting them apart and drawing the words at random from a hat (or box or whatever). To make a better review, you might ask for the definition and spelling of each word as you call it out–or you could call out the definitions and have students tell you the words they need to look for on the puzzle.

JUGGLE LETTERS
The vocabulary juggle letter game is intended to help students learn the spellings of the words. One sheet has the definitions listed on it as an extra help for students who need it or to reinforce the definitions if you choose to do so.

FLASH CARDS
We've included a set of vocabulary flash cards you can duplicate, cut, and fold for your students. Some teachers make a few sets for general use by the class; others make a set for each student. Some teachers duplicate them for each student and have the students cut & fold their own. You can cut out just the words and put them in a hat, have each student pick out one word and write the definition and a sentence for that word. Students then swap words and papers, with the next student adding a sentence of his own under the last one. You can have students swap as many times as you like. Each time the student will read the sentences written prior to his own and then add a sentence. You can cut out the words and definitions separately and play "I Have; Who Has?" Each student in the room draws a word and definition. The first student says, "I have (the name of the word). Who has the definition?" The student with the definition reads it then says, "I have (the name of the vocabulary word she has). Who has the definition?" The round continues until all words and definitions have been given.

Beowulf Unit Word List

No.	Word	Clue/Definition
1.	ALLEGORY	A story told on two levels
2.	ALLITERATION	Repetition of initial consonant sound
3.	ANONYMOUS	The Beowulf author
4.	ARISTOCRATIC	The Class of society that Beowulf is concerned with
5.	BOASTFUL	Adjective that describes Unferth
6.	CAIN	Person that Grendel and his mom were descended from
7.	CAVE	Place where Grendel and his mother dwelled
8.	CHRISTIAN	Influences that inserted God into this initially pagan text
9.	CLAW	Only part of Grendel left at Herot after the fight with Beowulf
10.	COWARDS	What Wiglaf calls Beowulf's soldiers
11.	CUP	Taken by slave from the dragon
12.	DENMARK	Hrothgar's homeland
13.	EDGETHO	Beowulf's father
14.	EPIC	Long, narrative poem
15.	ESHER	Hrothgar's best friend; killed by Grendel's mother
16.	FAME	The only thing that lasts, according to the Anglo-Saxons
17.	FEASTS	Large parties that celebrate battle victories
18.	FEUDAL	Times of the Anglo-Saxons
19.	FIRES	What almost destroyed the last manuscript of Beowulf
20.	GEATLAND	Beowulf's homeland
21.	GOD	Beowulf's inspiration
22.	HERO	Lead characer of an epic; the protagonist
23.	HEROT	Hrothgar's mead hall
24.	HIGD	Higlac's wife
25.	HIGLAC	King of the Geats at the beginning of the epic
26.	HILT	Handle of a sword or dagger
27.	HORSEMEN	They rode around Beowulf's grave
28.	HROTHGAR	King of the Danes
29.	HRUNTING	Name of Unferth's sword
30.	KENNING	Anglo-Saxon metaphor
31.	LAKE	Grendel and his mom live at the bottom of this
32.	MAIL	Protective chains worn by Beowulf
33.	MONKS	They first put Beowulf in written form
34.	OMENS	Signs which predict the future
35.	ORAL	Beowulf was first sung in this tradition
36.	PAGAN	Beowulf's heathen origins
37.	PRIDE	What Hrothgar cautions Beowulf against
38.	PYRE	Funeral fire
39.	RAFFEL	Translator of Beowulf
40.	RHYTHM	The beat or cadence of the lines in poetry
41.	SERPENTS	What Beowulf encountered and slew on the way to Grendel's mother
42.	SIEGMUND	Earlier hero who also killed a dragon
43.	SLAVE	Awakened the sleeping dragon
44.	SWIMMING	Beowulf defeats Brecca in this competition
45.	TREASURE	It was guarded by the dragon
46.	TRIPARTITE	3-part story, such as Beowulf
47.	UNFERTH	He challenged Beowulf's swimming prowess
48.	WARRIOR	Type of person most prized in Anglo-Saxon society
49.	WELTHOW	Hrothgar's queen
50.	WULFGAR	Swedish prince who introduced Beowulf to Hrothgar

Beowulf Fill In The Blank 1

_____ 1. Earlier hero who also killed a dragon

_____ 2. Translator of Beowulf

_____ 3. Times of the Anglo-Saxons

_____ 4. Influences that inserted God into this initially pagan text

_____ 5. Large parties that celebrate battle victories

_____ 6. Higlac's wife

_____ 7. What Hrothgar cautions Beowulf against

_____ 8. Protective chains worn by Beowulf

_____ 9. King of the Geats

_____ 10. Person that Grendel and his mom were descended from

_____ 11. Funeral fire

_____ 12. Beowulf's homeland

_____ 13. He challenged Beowulf's swimming prowess

_____ 14. Beowulf's father

_____ 15. Beowulf's inspiration

_____ 16. The Beowulf author

_____ 17. Adjective that describes Unferth

_____ 18. Type of person most prized in Anglo-Saxon society

_____ 19. Repetition of initial consonant sound

_____ 20. Anglo-Saxon metaphor

Beowulf Fill In The Blank 1 Answer Key

Answer	Clue
SIEGMUND	1. Earlier hero who also killed a dragon
RAFFEL	2. Translator of Beowulf
FEUDAL	3. Times of the Anglo-Saxons
CHRISTIAN	4. Influences that inserted God into this initially pagan text
FEASTS	5. Large parties that celebrate battle victories
HIGD	6. Higlac's wife
PRIDE	7. What Hrothgar cautions Beowulf against
MAIL	8. Protective chains worn by Beowulf
HROTHGAR	9. King of the Danes
CAIN	10. Person that Grendel and his mom were descended from
PYRE	11. Funeral fire
GEATLAND	12. Beowulf's homeland
UNFERTH	13. He challenged Beowulf's swimming prowess
EDGETHO	14. Beowulf's father
GOD	15. Beowulf's inspiration
ANONYMOUS	16. The Beowulf author
BOASTFUL	17. Adjective that describes Unferth
WARRIOR	18. Type of person most prized in Anglo-Saxon society
ALLITERATION	19. Repetition of initial consonant sound
KENNING	20. Anglo-Saxon metaphor

Beowulf Fill In The Blank 2

_____

_____

_____

_____

_____

_____

_____

_____

_____

_____

_____

_____

_____

_____

_____

_____

_____

_____

_____

_____

1. The Beowulf author
2. Name of Unferth's sword
3. Only part of Grendel left at Herot after the fight with Beowulf
4. Beowulf's father
5. Grendel and his mom live at the bottom of this
6. Higlac's wife
7. Beowulf's inspiration
8. Influences that inserted God into this initially pagan text
9. 3-part story, such as Beowulf
10. What Wiglaf calls Beowulf's soldiers
11. Beowulf defeats Brecca in this competition
12. Swedish prince who introduced Beowulf to Hrothgar
13. Long, narrative poem
14. Signs which predict the future
15. Type of person most prized in Anglo-Saxon society
16. What almost destroyed the last manuscript of Beowulf
17. Lead characer of an epic; the protagonist
18. The Class of society that Beowulf is concerned with
19. Anglo-Saxon metaphor
20. Hrothgar's mead hall

Beowulf Fill In The Blank 2 Answer Key

ANONYMOUS	1. The Beowulf author
HRUNTING	2. Name of Unferth's sword
CLAW	3. Only part of Grendel left at Herot after the fight with Beowulf
EDGETHO	4. Beowulf's father
LAKE	5. Grendel and his mom live at the bottom of this
HIGD	6. Higlac's wife
GOD	7. Beowulf's inspiration
CHRISTIAN	8. Influences that inserted God into this initially pagan text
TRIPARTITE	9. 3-part story, such as Beowulf
COWARDS	10. What Wiglaf calls Beowulf's soldiers
SWIMMING	11. Beowulf defeats Brecca in this competition
WULFGAR	12. Swedish prince who introduced Beowulf to Hrothgar
EPIC	13. Long, narrative poem
OMENS	14. Signs which predict the future
WARRIOR	15. Type of person most prized in Anglo-Saxon society
FIRES	16. What almost destroyed the last manuscript of Beowulf
HERO	17. Lead characer of an epic; the protagonist
ARISTOCRATIC	18. The Class of society that Beowulf is concerned with
KENNING	19. Anglo-Saxon metaphor
HEROT	20. Hrothgar's mead hall

Beowulf Fill In The Blank 3

_____ 1. 3-part story, such as Beowulf

_____ 2. Taken by slave from the dragon

_____ 3. Adjective that describes Unferth

_____ 4. Name of Unferth's sword

_____ 5. Beowulf's inspiration

_____ 6. He challenged Beowulf's swimming prowess

_____ 7. Repetition of initial consonant sound

_____ 8. Times of the Anglo-Saxons

_____ 9. Beowulf's heathen origins

_____ 10. The beat or cadence of the lines in poetry

_____ 11. Handle of a sword or dagger

_____ 12. King of the Geats

_____ 13. King of the Geats at the beginning of the epic

_____ 14. Large parties that celebrate battle victories

_____ 15. Beowulf was first sung in this tradition

_____ 16. What Beowulf encountered and slew on the way to Grendel's mother

_____ 17. Signs which predict the future

_____ 18. Lead characer of an epic; the protagonist

_____ 19. Beowulf defeats Brecca in this competition

_____ 20. Funeral fire

Beowulf Fill In The Blank 3 Answer Key

TRIPARTITE	1. 3-part story, such as Beowulf
CUP	2. Taken by slave from the dragon
BOASTFUL	3. Adjective that describes Unferth
HRUNTING	4. Name of Unferth's sword
GOD	5. Beowulf's inspiration
UNFERTH	6. He challenged Beowulf's swimming prowess
ALLITERATION	7. Repetition of initial consonant sound
FEUDAL	8. Times of the Anglo-Saxons
PAGAN	9. Beowulf's heathen origins
RHYTHM	10. The beat or cadence of the lines in poetry
HILT	11. Handle of a sword or dagger
HROTHGAR	12. King of the Danes
HIGLAC	13. King of the Geats at the beginning of the epic
FEASTS	14. Large parties that celebrate battle victories
ORAL	15. Beowulf was first sung in this tradition
SERPENTS	16. What Beowulf encountered and slew on the way to Grendel's mother
OMENS	17. Signs which predict the future
HERO	18. Lead characer of an epic; the protagonist
SWIMMING	19. Beowulf defeats Brecca in this competition
PYRE	20. Funeral fire

Beowulf Fill In The Blank 4

_____
_____
_____
_____
_____
_____
_____
_____
_____
_____
_____
_____
_____
_____
_____
_____
_____
_____
_____
_____

1. Hrothgar's mead hall
2. Beowulf was first sung in this tradition
3. He challenged Beowulf's swimming prowess
4. Handle of a sword or dagger
5. Swedish prince who introduced Beowulf to Hrothgar
6. What Wiglaf calls Beowulf's soldiers
7. The Class of society that Beowulf is concerned with
8. Beowulf's inspiration
9. Adjective that describes Unferth
10. Earlier hero who also killed a dragon
11. Higlac's wife
12. What Beowulf encountered and slew on the way to Grendel's mother
13. The Beowulf author
14. Translator of Beowulf
15. Beowulf's father
16. Beowulf's heathen origins
17. What Hrothgar cautions Beowulf against
18. Hrothgar's queen
19. Beowulf's homeland
20. It was guarded by the dragon

Beowulf Fill In The Blank 4 Answer Key

HEROT	1. Hrothgar's mead hall
ORAL	2. Beowulf was first sung in this tradition
UNFERTH	3. He challenged Beowulf's swimming prowess
HILT	4. Handle of a sword or dagger
WULFGAR	5. Swedish prince who introduced Beowulf to Hrothgar
COWARDS	6. What Wiglaf calls Beowulf's soldiers
ARISTOCRATIC	7. The Class of society that Beowulf is concerned with
GOD	8. Beowulf's inspiration
BOASTFUL	9. Adjective that describes Unferth
SIEGMUND	10. Earlier hero who also killed a dragon
HIGD	11. Higlac's wife
SERPENTS	12. What Beowulf encountered and slew on the way to Grendel's mother
ANONYMOUS	13. The Beowulf author
RAFFEL	14. Translator of Beowulf
EDGETHO	15. Beowulf's father
PAGAN	16. Beowulf's heathen origins
PRIDE	17. What Hrothgar cautions Beowulf against
WELTHOW	18. Hrothgar's queen
GEATLAND	19. Beowulf's homeland
TREASURE	20. It was guarded by the dragon

Beowulf Matching 1

___ 1. WELTHOW   A. Signs which predict the future
___ 2. MAIL   B. The beat or cadence of the lines in poetry
___ 3. HIGD   C. Hrothgar's mead hall
___ 4. WULFGAR   D. Hrothgar's queen
___ 5. SLAVE   E. Beowulf's inspiration
___ 6. EPIC   F. Repetition of initial consonant sound
___ 7. ALLEGORY   G. Handle of a sword or dagger
___ 8. FEASTS   H. King of the Geats at the beginning of the epic
___ 9. PRIDE   I. It was guarded by the dragon
___10. GEATLAND   J. Higlac's wife
___11. EDGETHO   K. A story told on two levels
___12. HIGLAC   L. Name of Unferth's sword
___13. HILT   M. Long, narrative poem
___14. RHYTHM   N. Place where Grendel and his mother dwelled
___15. KENNING   O. Anglo-Saxon metaphor
___16. HORSEMEN   P. Translator of Beowulf
___17. GOD   Q. Large parties that celebrate battle victories
___18. ALLITERATION   R. What Hrothgar cautions Beowulf against
___19. RAFFEL   S. They rode around Beowulf's grave
___20. CAVE   T. Beowulf's homeland
___21. TREASURE   U. Protective chains worn by Beowulf
___22. WARRIOR   V. Swedish prince who introduced Beowulf to Hrothgar
___23. HRUNTING   W. Beowulf's father
___24. HEROT   X. Awakened the sleeping dragon
___25. OMENS   Y. Type of person most prized in Anglo-Saxon society

Beowulf Matching 1 Answer Key

D - 1. WELTHOW	A.	Signs which predict the future
U - 2. MAIL	B.	The beat or cadence of the lines in poetry
J - 3. HIGD	C.	Hrothgar's mead hall
V - 4. WULFGAR	D.	Hrothgar's queen
X - 5. SLAVE	E.	Beowulf's inspiration
M - 6. EPIC	F.	Repetition of initial consonant sound
K - 7. ALLEGORY	G.	Handle of a sword or dagger
Q - 8. FEASTS	H.	King of the Geats at the beginning of the epic
R - 9. PRIDE	I.	It was guarded by the dragon
T - 10. GEATLAND	J.	Higlac's wife
W - 11. EDGETHO	K.	A story told on two levels
H - 12. HIGLAC	L.	Name of Unferth's sword
G - 13. HILT	M.	Long, narrative poem
B - 14. RHYTHM	N.	Place where Grendel and his mother dwelled
O - 15. KENNING	O.	Anglo-Saxon metaphor
S - 16. HORSEMEN	P.	Translator of Beowulf
E - 17. GOD	Q.	Large parties that celebrate battle victories
F - 18. ALLITERATION	R.	What Hrothgar cautions Beowulf against
P - 19. RAFFEL	S.	They rode around Beowulf's grave
N - 20. CAVE	T.	Beowulf's homeland
I - 21. TREASURE	U.	Protective chains worn by Beowulf
Y - 22. WARRIOR	V.	Swedish prince who introduced Beowulf to Hrothgar
L - 23. HRUNTING	W.	Beowulf's father
C - 24. HEROT	X.	Awakened the sleeping dragon
A - 25. OMENS	Y.	Type of person most prized in Anglo-Saxon society

Beowulf Matching 2

___ 1. SERPENTS	A. Higlac's wife
___ 2. TREASURE	B. Signs which predict the future
___ 3. UNFERTH	C. Only part of Grendel left at Herot after the fight with Beowulf
___ 4. CLAW	D. Type of person most prized in Anglo-Saxon society
___ 5. WULFGAR	E. The only thing that lasts, according to the Anglo-Saxons
___ 6. WARRIOR	F. Place where Grendel and his mother dwelled
___ 7. OMENS	G. Translator of Beowulf
___ 8. MAIL	H. The beat or cadence of the lines in poetry
___ 9. SIEGMUND	I. They rode around Beowulf's grave
___ 10. ARISTOCRATIC	J. The Class of society that Beowulf is concerned with
___ 11. PYRE	K. Beowulf's homeland
___ 12. RHYTHM	L. Large parties that celebrate battle victories
___ 13. EDGETHO	M. Earlier hero who also killed a dragon
___ 14. GEATLAND	N. He challenged Beowulf's swimming prowess
___ 15. FAME	O. What Beowulf encountered and slew on the way to Grendel's mother
___ 16. CAVE	P. Swedish prince who introduced Beowulf to Hrothgar
___ 17. HORSEMEN	Q. King of the Geats at the beginning of the epic
___ 18. FEASTS	R. It was guarded by the dragon
___ 19. PAGAN	S. Protective chains worn by Beowulf
___ 20. COWARDS	T. What Wiglaf calls Beowulf's soldiers
___ 21. HIGLAC	U. Person that Grendel and his mom were descended from
___ 22. RAFFEL	V. Funeral fire
___ 23. CAIN	W. Beowulf's father
___ 24. HIGD	X. Beowulf was first sung in this tradition
___ 25. ORAL	Y. Beowulf's heathen origins

Beowulf Matching 2 Answer Key

O - 1. SERPENTS	A.	Higlac's wife
R - 2. TREASURE	B.	Signs which predict the future
N - 3. UNFERTH	C.	Only part of Grendel left at Herot after the fight with Beowulf
C - 4. CLAW	D.	Type of person most prized in Anglo-Saxon society
P - 5. WULFGAR	E.	The only thing that lasts, according to the Anglo-Saxons
D - 6. WARRIOR	F.	Place where Grendel and his mother dwelled
B - 7. OMENS	G.	Translator of Beowulf
S - 8. MAIL	H.	The beat or cadence of the lines in poetry
M - 9. SIEGMUND	I.	They rode around Beowulf's grave
J - 10. ARISTOCRATIC	J.	The Class of society that Beowulf is concerned with
V - 11. PYRE	K.	Beowulf's homeland
H - 12. RHYTHM	L.	Large parties that celebrate battle victories
W - 13. EDGETHO	M.	Earlier hero who also killed a dragon
K - 14. GEATLAND	N.	He challenged Beowulf's swimming prowess
E - 15. FAME	O.	What Beowulf encountered and slew on the way to Grendel's mother
F - 16. CAVE	P.	Swedish prince who introduced Beowulf to Hrothgar
I - 17. HORSEMEN	Q.	King of the Geats at the beginning of the epic
L - 18. FEASTS	R.	It was guarded by the dragon
Y - 19. PAGAN	S.	Protective chains worn by Beowulf
T - 20. COWARDS	T.	What Wiglaf calls Beowulf's soldiers
Q - 21. HIGLAC	U.	Person that Grendel and his mom were descended from
G - 22. RAFFEL	V.	Funeral fire
U - 23. CAIN	W.	Beowulf's father
A - 24. HIGD	X.	Beowulf was first sung in this tradition
X - 25. ORAL	Y.	Beowulf's heathen origins

Beowulf Matching 3

___ 1. GEATLAND   A. Large parties that celebrate battle victories
___ 2. LAKE   B. Type of person most prized in Anglo-Saxon society
___ 3. PAGAN   C. Handle of a sword or dagger
___ 4. CAIN   D. He challenged Beowulf's swimming prowess
___ 5. ANONYMOUS   E. Hrothgar's mead hall
___ 6. HEROT   F. What Wiglaf calls Beowulf's soldiers
___ 7. FEUDAL   G. Beowulf's homeland
___ 8. FEASTS   H. Beowulf's heathen origins
___ 9. HIGD   I. The Beowulf author
___10. FAME   J. Long, narrative poem
___11. HRUNTING   K. Grendel and his mom live at the bottom of this
___12. SERPENTS   L. Awakened the sleeping dragon
___13. ARISTOCRATIC   M. They rode around Beowulf's grave
___14. ALLITERATION   N. They first put Beowulf in written form
___15. WARRIOR   O. Beowulf's father
___16. EDGETHO   P. Times of the Anglo-Saxons
___17. SLAVE   Q. A story told on two levels
___18. CHRISTIAN   R. The only thing that lasts, according to the Anglo-Saxons
___19. HORSEMEN   S. Person that Grendel and his mom were descended from
___20. MONKS   T. The Class of society that Beowulf is concerned with
___21. UNFERTH   U. Higlac's wife
___22. COWARDS   V. Name of Unferth's sword
___23. HILT   W. Influences that inserted God into this initially pagan text
___24. ALLEGORY   X. What Beowulf encountered and slew on the way to Grendel's mother
___25. EPIC   Y. Repetition of initial consonant sound

Beowulf Matching 3 Answer Key

G - 1. GEATLAND	A.	Large parties that celebrate battle victories
K - 2. LAKE	B.	Type of person most prized in Anglo-Saxon society
H - 3. PAGAN	C.	Handle of a sword or dagger
S - 4. CAIN	D.	He challenged Beowulf's swimming prowess
I - 5. ANONYMOUS	E.	Hrothgar's mead hall
E - 6. HEROT	F.	What Wiglaf calls Beowulf's soldiers
P - 7. FEUDAL	G.	Beowulf's homeland
A - 8. FEASTS	H.	Beowulf's heathen origins
U - 9. HIGD	I.	The Beowulf author
R -10. FAME	J.	Long, narrative poem
V -11. HRUNTING	K.	Grendel and his mom live at the bottom of this
X -12. SERPENTS	L.	Awakened the sleeping dragon
T -13. ARISTOCRATIC	M.	They rode around Beowulf's grave
Y -14. ALLITERATION	N.	They first put Beowulf in written form
B -15. WARRIOR	O.	Beowulf's father
O -16. EDGETHO	P.	Times of the Anglo-Saxons
L -17. SLAVE	Q.	A story told on two levels
W -18. CHRISTIAN	R.	The only thing that lasts, according to the Anglo-Saxons
M -19. HORSEMEN	S.	Person that Grendel and his mom were descended from
N -20. MONKS	T.	The Class of society that Beowulf is concerned with
D -21. UNFERTH	U.	Higlac's wife
F -22. COWARDS	V.	Name of Unferth's sword
C -23. HILT	W.	Influences that inserted God into this initially pagan text
Q -24. ALLEGORY	X.	What Beowulf encountered and slew on the way to Grendel's mother
J - 25. EPIC	Y.	Repetition of initial consonant sound

Beowulf Matching 4

___ 1. ALLITERATION A. Place where Grendel and his mother dwelled
___ 2. HILT B. Long, narrative poem
___ 3. FEUDAL C. Higlac's wife
___ 4. CAVE D. What Beowulf encountered and slew on the way to Grendel's mother
___ 5. ESHER E. He challenged Beowulf's swimming prowess
___ 6. DENMARK F. Times of the Anglo-Saxons
___ 7. EPIC G. Beowulf was first sung in this tradition
___ 8. CUP H. A story told on two levels
___ 9. HRUNTING I. Taken by slave from the dragon
___ 10. GOD J. Beowulf's inspiration
___ 11. CHRISTIAN K. Hrothgar's best friend; killed by Grendel's mother
___ 12. SWIMMING L. Handle of a sword or dagger
___ 13. FAME M. Beowulf's heathen origins
___ 14. BOASTFUL N. Name of Unferth's sword
___ 15. SIEGMUND O. Adjective that describes Unferth
___ 16. ORAL P. Hrothgar's mead hall
___ 17. TREASURE Q. Funeral fire
___ 18. ANONYMOUS R. It was guarded by the dragon
___ 19. PAGAN S. Hrothgar's homeland
___ 20. UNFERTH T. Influences that inserted God into this initially pagan text
___ 21. ALLEGORY U. Earlier hero who also killed a dragon
___ 22. HIGD V. The Beowulf author
___ 23. PYRE W. Beowulf defeats Brecca in this competition
___ 24. SERPENTS X. Repetition of initial consonant sound
___ 25. HEROT Y. The only thing that lasts, according to the Anglo-Saxons

Beowulf Matching 4 Answer Key

X - 1.	ALLITERATION	A.	Place where Grendel and his mother dwelled
L - 2.	HILT	B.	Long, narrative poem
F - 3.	FEUDAL	C.	Higlac's wife
A - 4.	CAVE	D.	What Beowulf encountered and slew on the way to Grendel's mother
K - 5.	ESHER	E.	He challenged Beowulf's swimming prowess
S - 6.	DENMARK	F.	Times of the Anglo-Saxons
B - 7.	EPIC	G.	Beowulf was first sung in this tradition
I - 8.	CUP	H.	A story told on two levels
N - 9.	HRUNTING	I.	Taken by slave from the dragon
J - 10.	GOD	J.	Beowulf's inspiration
T - 11.	CHRISTIAN	K.	Hrothgar's best friend; killed by Grendel's mother
W - 12.	SWIMMING	L.	Handle of a sword or dagger
Y - 13.	FAME	M.	Beowulf's heathen origins
O - 14.	BOASTFUL	N.	Name of Unferth's sword
U - 15.	SIEGMUND	O.	Adjective that describes Unferth
G - 16.	ORAL	P.	Hrothgar's mead hall
R - 17.	TREASURE	Q.	Funeral fire
V - 18.	ANONYMOUS	R.	It was guarded by the dragon
M - 19.	PAGAN	S.	Hrothgar's homeland
E - 20.	UNFERTH	T.	Influences that inserted God into this initially pagan text
H - 21.	ALLEGORY	U.	Earlier hero who also killed a dragon
C - 22.	HIGD	V.	The Beowulf author
Q - 23.	PYRE	W.	Beowulf defeats Brecca in this competition
D - 24.	SERPENTS	X.	Repetition of initial consonant sound
P - 25.	HEROT	Y.	The only thing that lasts, according to the Anglo-Saxons

Beowulf Magic Squares 1

Match the definition with the vocabulary word. Put your answers in the magic squares below. When your answers are correct, all columns and rows will add to the same number.

A. HIGD
B. FIRES
C. PYRE
D. GEATLAND
E. CAVE
F. TRIPARTITE
G. RAFFEL
H. CUP
I. COWARDS
J. HORSEMEN
K. ESHER
L. CLAW
M. PRIDE
N. SIEGMUND
O. UNFERTH
P. DENMARK

1. What Hrothgar cautions Beowulf against
2. 3-part story, such as Beowulf
3. Taken by slave from the dragon
4. He challenged Beowulf's swimming prowess
5. Only part of Grendel left at Herot after the fight with Beowulf
6. Funeral fire
7. Higlac's wife
8. They rode around Beowulf's grave
9. Hrothgar's best friend; killed by Grendel's mother
10. Beowulf's homeland
11. What almost destroyed the last manuscript of Beowulf
12. What Wiglaf calls Beowulf's soldiers
13. Earlier hero who also killed a dragon
14. Place where Grendel and his mother dwelled
15. Translator of Beowulf
16. Hrothgar's homeland

A=	B=	C=	D=
E=	F=	G=	H=
I=	J=	K=	L=
M=	N=	O=	P=

Beowulf Magic Sqares 1 Answer Key

Match the definition with the vocabulary word. Put your answers in the magic squares below. When your answers are correct, all columns and rows will add to the same number.

A. HIGD
B. FIRES
C. PYRE
D. GEATLAND
E. CAVE
F. TRIPARTITE
G. RAFFEL
H. CUP
I. COWARDS
J. HORSEMEN
K. ESHER
L. CLAW
M. PRIDE
N. SIEGMUND
O. UNFERTH
P. DENMARK

1. What Hrothgar cautions Beowulf against
2. 3-part story, such as Beowulf
3. Taken by slave from the dragon
4. He challenged Beowulf's swimming prowess
5. Only part of Grendel left at Herot after the fight with Beowulf
6. Funeral fire
7. Higlac's wife
8. They rode around Beowulf's grave
9. Hrothgar's best friend; killed by Grendel's mother
10. Beowulf's homeland
11. What almost destroyed the last manuscript of Beowulf
12. What Wiglaf calls Beowulf's soldiers
13. Earlier hero who also killed a dragon
14. Place where Grendel and his mother dwelled
15. Translator of Beowulf
16. Hrothgar's homeland

A=7	B=11	C=6	D=10
E=14	F=2	G=15	H=3
I=12	J=8	K=9	L=5
M=1	N=13	O=4	P=16

Beowulf Magic Squares 2

Match the definition with the vocabulary word. Put your answers in the magic squares below. When your answers are correct, all columns and rows will add to the same number.

A. TRIPARTITE
B. MAIL
C. OMENS
D. FEASTS
E. CUP
F. FEUDAL
G. CHRISTIAN
H. SIEGMUND
I. HIGD
J. HROTHGAR
K. ARISTOCRATIC
L. RHYTHM
M. EDGETHO
N. COWARDS
O. LAKE
P. WULFGAR

1. Grendel and his mom live at the bottom of this
2. King of the Danes
3. Earlier hero who also killed a dragon
4. 3-part story, such as Beowulf
5. Large parties that celebrate battle victories
6. Taken by slave from the dragon
7. The Class of society that Beowulf is concerned with
8. What Wiglaf calls Beowulf's soldiers
9. Times of the Anglo-Saxons
10. Signs which predict the future
11. Beowulf's father
12. The beat or cadence of the lines in poetry
13. Higlac's wife
14. Swedish prince who introduced Beowulf to Hrothgar
15. Protective chains worn by Beowulf
16. Influences that inserted God into this initially pagan text

A=	B=	C=	D=
E=	F=	G=	H=
I=	J=	K=	L=
M=	N=	O=	P=

Beowulf Magic Squares 2 Answer Key

Match the definition with the vocabulary word. Put your answers in the magic squares below. When your answers are correct, all columns and rows will add to the same number.

A. TRIPARTITE
B. MAIL
C. OMENS
D. FEASTS
E. CUP
F. FEUDAL
G. CHRISTIAN
H. SIEGMUND
I. HIGD
J. HROTHGAR
K. ARISTOCRATIC
L. RHYTHM
M. EDGETHO
N. COWARDS
O. LAKE
P. WULFGAR

1. Grendel and his mom live at the bottom of this
2. King of the Danes
3. Earlier hero who also killed a dragon
4. 3-part story, such as Beowulf
5. Large parties that celebrate battle victories
6. Taken by slave from the dragon
7. The Class of society that Beowulf is concerned with
8. What Wiglaf calls Beowulf's soldiers
9. Times of the Anglo-Saxons
10. Signs which predict the future
11. Beowulf's father
12. The beat or cadence of the lines in poetry
13. Higlac's wife
14. Swedish prince who introduced Beowulf to Hrothgar
15. Protective chains worn by Beowulf
16. Influences that inserted God into this initially pagan text

A=4	B=15	C=10	D=5
E=6	F=9	G=16	H=3
I=13	J=2	K=7	L=12
M=11	N=8	O=1	P=14

Beowulf Magic Squares 3

Match the definition with the vocabulary word. Put your answers in the magic squares below. When your answers are correct, all columns and rows will add to the same number.

A. HIGLAC
B. KENNING
C. SLAVE
D. HROTHGAR
E. WELTHOW
F. UNFERTH
G. SWIMMING
H. PYRE
I. FAME
J. COWARDS
K. DENMARK
L. WULFGAR
M. PRIDE
N. HILT
O. HORSEMEN
P. HIGD

1. They rode around Beowulf's grave
2. King of the Danes
3. What Wiglaf calls Beowulf's soldiers
4. Hrothgar's queen
5. The only thing that lasts, according to the Anglo-Saxons
6. He challenged Beowulf's swimming prowess
7. Higlac's wife
8. Awakened the sleeping dragon
9. Funeral fire
10. Hrothgar's homeland
11. King of the Geats at the beginning of the epic
12. Handle of a sword or dagger
13. Anglo-Saxon metaphor
14. What Hrothgar cautions Beowulf against
15. Beowulf defeats Brecca in this competition
16. Swedish prince who introduced Beowulf to Hrothgar

A=	B=	C=	D=
E=	F=	G=	H=
I=	J=	K=	L=
M=	N=	O=	P=

Beowulf Magic Squares 3 Answer Key

Match the definition with the vocabulary word. Put your answers in the magic squares below. When your answers are correct, all columns and rows will add to the same number.

A. HIGLAC
B. KENNING
C. SLAVE
D. HROTHGAR
E. WELTHOW
F. UNFERTH
G. SWIMMING
H. PYRE
I. FAME
J. COWARDS
K. DENMARK
L. WULFGAR
M. PRIDE
N. HILT
O. HORSEMEN
P. HIGD

1. They rode around Beowulf's grave
2. King of the Danes
3. What Wiglaf calls Beowulf's soldiers
4. Hrothgar's queen
5. The only thing that lasts, according to the Anglo-Saxons
6. He challenged Beowulf's swimming prowess
7. Higlac's wife
8. Awakened the sleeping dragon
9. Funeral fire
10. Hrothgar's homeland
11. King of the Geats at the beginning of the epic
12. Handle of a sword or dagger
13. Anglo-Saxon metaphor
14. What Hrothgar cautions Beowulf against
15. Beowulf defeats Brecca in this competition
16. Swedish prince who introduced Beowulf to Hrothgar

A=11	B=13	C=8	D=2
E=4	F=6	G=15	H=9
I=5	J=3	K=10	L=16
M=14	N=12	O=1	P=7

Beowulf Magic Squares 4

Match the definition with the vocabulary word. Put your answers in the magic squares below. When your answers are correct, all columns and rows will add to the same number.

A. SERPENTS
B. HEROT
C. GOD
D. FEASTS
E. HRUNTING
F. PYRE
G. FEUDAL
H. EPIC
I. SIEGMUND
J. CAVE
K. CLAW
L. RAFFEL
M. MONKS
N. FAME
O. COWARDS
P. HROTHGAR

1. Funeral fire
2. Earlier hero who also killed a dragon
3. What Wiglaf calls Beowulf's soldiers
4. Large parties that celebrate battle victories
5. They first put Beowulf in written form
6. Hrothgar's mead hall
7. Long, narrative poem
8. Only part of Grendel left at Herot after the fight with Beowulf
9. Beowulf's inspiration
10. King of the Danes
11. Place where Grendel and his mother dwelled
12. Name of Unferth's sword
13. Translator of Beowulf
14. Times of the Anglo-Saxons
15. What Beowulf encountered and slew on the way to Grendel's mother
16. The only thing that lasts, according to the Anglo-Saxons

A=	B=	C=	D=
E=	F=	G=	H=
I=	J=	K=	L=
M=	N=	O=	P=

Beowulf Magic Squares 4 Answer Key

Match the definition with the vocabulary word. Put your answers in the magic squares below. When your answers are correct, all columns and rows will add to the same number.

A. SERPENTS
B. HEROT
C. GOD
D. FEASTS
E. HRUNTING
F. PYRE
G. FEUDAL
H. EPIC
I. SIEGMUND
J. CAVE
K. CLAW
L. RAFFEL
M. MONKS
N. FAME
O. COWARDS
P. HROTHGAR

1. Funeral fire
2. Earlier hero who also killed a dragon
3. What Wiglaf calls Beowulf's soldiers
4. Large parties that celebrate battle victories
5. They first put Beowulf in written form
6. Hrothgar's mead hall
7. Long, narrative poem
8. Only part of Grendel left at Herot after the fight with Beowulf
9. Beowulf's inspiration
10. King of the Danes
11. Place where Grendel and his mother dwelled
12. Name of Unferth's sword
13. Translator of Beowulf
14. Times of the Anglo-Saxons
15. What Beowulf encountered and slew on the way to Grendel's mother
16. The only thing that lasts, according to the Anglo-Saxons

A=15	B=6	C=9	D=4
E=12	F=1	G=14	H=7
I=2	J=11	K=8	L=13
M=5	N=16	O=3	P=10

Beowulf Word Search 1

```
H S T N E P R E S J Q E S S F S P
E F E A S T S V X E Q D M L G C R
R F H H H N H R G K Z G K E A K I
O L H E E T R P C A W E A G K V D
T R O I R R A W A L C T R P Y R E
C M Z E R O O L A M L H I K W M L
U P F K B H F D A A C O S D A O W
P N B C T C U I N H R S T F E M Y
U K N L O E L D R A S I O N T E R
H P E C F W S L G E C E C Q I N A
R W M H C Y A F P O S G R O T S F
U K E V A C L R N R D M A J R C F
N W S L K U Q A D L B U T H A A E
T T R B W W G W P S F N I H P I L
I B O P B A M O N K S D C I I N B
N C H B P T R E A S U R E G R L J
G E P I C D E N M A R K Y D T M T
```

3-part story, such as Beowulf (10)
Awakened the sleeping dragon (5)
Beowulf was first sung in this tradition (4)
Beowulf's father (7)
Beowulf's heathen origins (5)
Beowulf's homeland (8)
Beowulf's inspiration (3)
Earlier hero who also killed a dragon (8)
Funeral fire (4)
Grendel and his mom live at the bottom of this (4)
Handle of a sword or dagger (4)
He challenged Beowulf's swimming prowess (7)
Higlac's wife (4)
Hrothgar's best friend; killed by Grendel's mother (5)
Hrothgar's homeland (7)
Hrothgar's mead hall (5)
Hrothgar's queen (7)
It was guarded by the dragon (8)
Large parties that celebrate battle victories (6)
Lead characer of an epic; the protagonist (4)
Long, narrative poem (4)
Name of Unferth's sword (8)

Only part of Grendel left at Herot after the fight with Beowulf (4)
Person that Grendel and his mom were descended from (4)
Place where Grendel and his mother dwelled (4)
Protective chains worn by Beowulf (4)
Signs which predict the future (5)
Swedish prince who introduced Beowulf to Hrothgar (7)
Taken by slave from the dragon (3)
The Class of society that Beowulf is concerned with (12)
The only thing that lasts, according to the Anglo-Saxons (4)
They first put Beowulf in written form (5)
They rode around Beowulf's grave (8)
Times of the Anglo-Saxons (6)
Translator of Beowulf (6)
Type of person most prized in Anglo-Saxon society (7)
What Beowulf encountered and slew on the way to Grendel's mother (8)
What Hrothgar cautions Beowulf against (5)
What Wiglaf calls Beowulf's soldiers (7)
What almost destroyed the last manuscript of Beowulf (5)

Beowulf Word Search 1 Answer Key

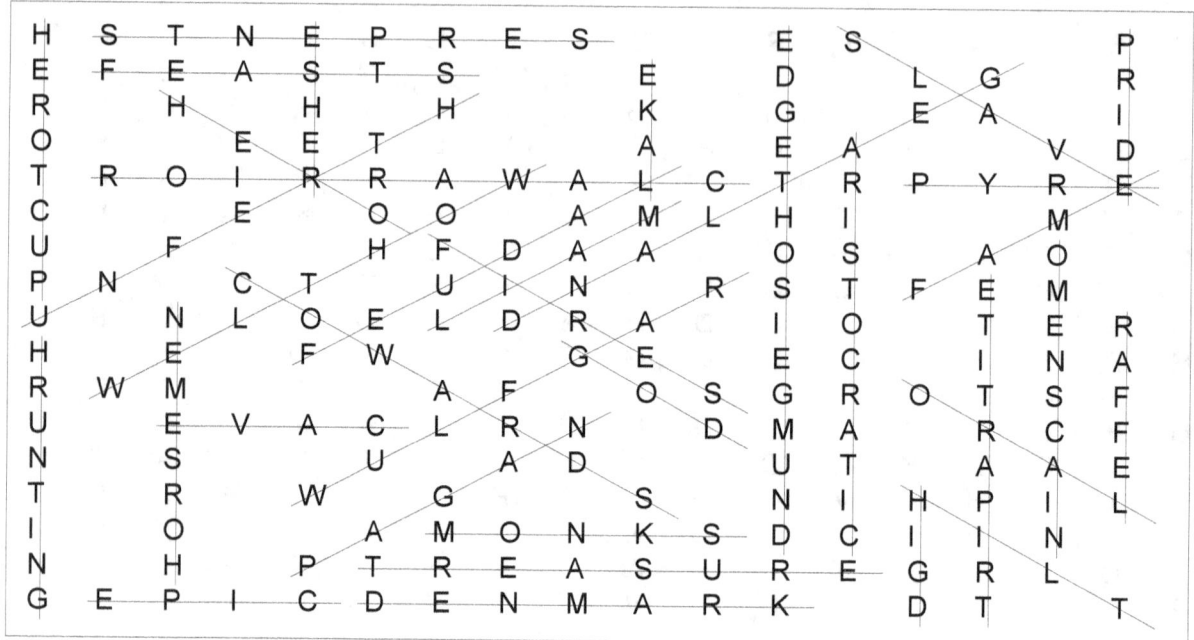

3-part story, such as Beowulf (10)
Awakened the sleeping dragon (5)
Beowulf was first sung in this tradition (4)
Beowulf's father (7)
Beowulf's heathen origins (5)
Beowulf's homeland (8)
Beowulf's inspiration (3)
Earlier hero who also killed a dragon (8)
Funeral fire (4)
Grendel and his mom live at the bottom of this (4)
Handle of a sword or dagger (4)
He challenged Beowulf's swimming prowess (7)
Higlac's wife (4)
Hrothgar's best friend; killed by Grendel's mother (5)
Hrothgar's homeland (7)
Hrothgar's mead hall (5)
Hrothgar's queen (7)
It was guarded by the dragon (8)
Large parties that celebrate battle victories (6)
Lead characer of an epic; the protagonist (4)
Long, narrative poem (4)
Name of Unferth's sword (8)

Only part of Grendel left at Herot after the fight with Beowulf (4)
Person that Grendel and his mom were descended from (4)
Place where Grendel and his mother dwelled (4)
Protective chains worn by Beowulf (4)
Signs which predict the future (5)
Swedish prince who introduced Beowulf to Hrothgar (7)
Taken by slave from the dragon (3)
The Class of society that Beowulf is concerned with (12)
The only thing that lasts, according to the Anglo-Saxons (4)
They first put Beowulf in written form (5)
They rode around Beowulf's grave (8)
Times of the Anglo-Saxons (6)
Translator of Beowulf (6)
Type of person most prized in Anglo-Saxon society (7)
What Beowulf encountered and slew on the way to Grendel's mother (8)
What Hrothgar cautions Beowulf against (5)
What Wiglaf calls Beowulf's soldiers (7)
What almost destroyed the last manuscript of Beowulf (5)

Beowulf Word Search 2

```
E P A G A N G C S W F F G M C F F
G D S C M O L T A X E E E D A U Z
A R G X H A R W R V N L A U S I P
K N X E W F C A J R E R T S D S L
E R O Y T A H R L E R S R H T A P
N H C N L H X R T H M B Y N O S L
N Y V G Y C O I D S L Z E R L W L
I T I O Y M T O S E X P S L A V E
N H M W M R O R V T R K W Y D B H
G M H R A E N U H E K B R S O D O
E R Y P M O N K S H R O T H G A R
W D I C T D R S Q A G A J I C H S
F R F W R A T D F E X S H M E D E
T I D P M O E F L P N T T R P D M
L N R N R K E L P I S F O J I Z E
I Z E E A L A Q A C J U K R C H N
H D H L S M V C Z C S L P F A M E
```

3-part story, such as Beowulf (10)
A story told on two levels (8)
Adjective that describes Unferth (8)
Anglo-Saxon metaphor (7)
Awakened the sleeping dragon (5)
Beowulf was first sung in this tradition (4)
Beowulf's father (7)
Beowulf's heathen origins (5)
Beowulf's inspiration (3)
Funeral fire (4)
Grendel and his mom live at the bottom of this (4)
Handle of a sword or dagger (4)
Higlac's wife (4)
Hrothgar's best friend; killed by Grendel's mother (5)
Hrothgar's homeland (7)
Hrothgar's mead hall (5)
Hrothgar's queen (7)
King of the Danes (8)
King of the Geats at the beginning of the epic (6)
Large parties that celebrate battle victories (6)
Lead characer of an epic; the protagonist (4)
Long, narrative poem (4)

Only part of Grendel left at Herot after the fight with Beowulf (4)
Person that Grendel and his mom were descended from (4)
Place where Grendel and his mother dwelled (4)
Protective chains worn by Beowulf (4)
Signs which predict the future (5)
Taken by slave from the dragon (3)
The Beowulf author (9)
The beat or cadence of the lines in poetry (6)
The only thing that lasts, according to the Anglo-Saxons (4)
They first put Beowulf in written form (5)
They rode around Beowulf's grave (8)
Times of the Anglo-Saxons (6)
Translator of Beowulf (6)
Type of person most prized in Anglo-Saxon society (7)
What Beowulf encountered and slew on the way to Grendel's mother (8)
What Hrothgar cautions Beowulf against (5)
What almost destroyed the last manuscript of Beowulf (5)

Beowulf Word Search 2 Answer Key

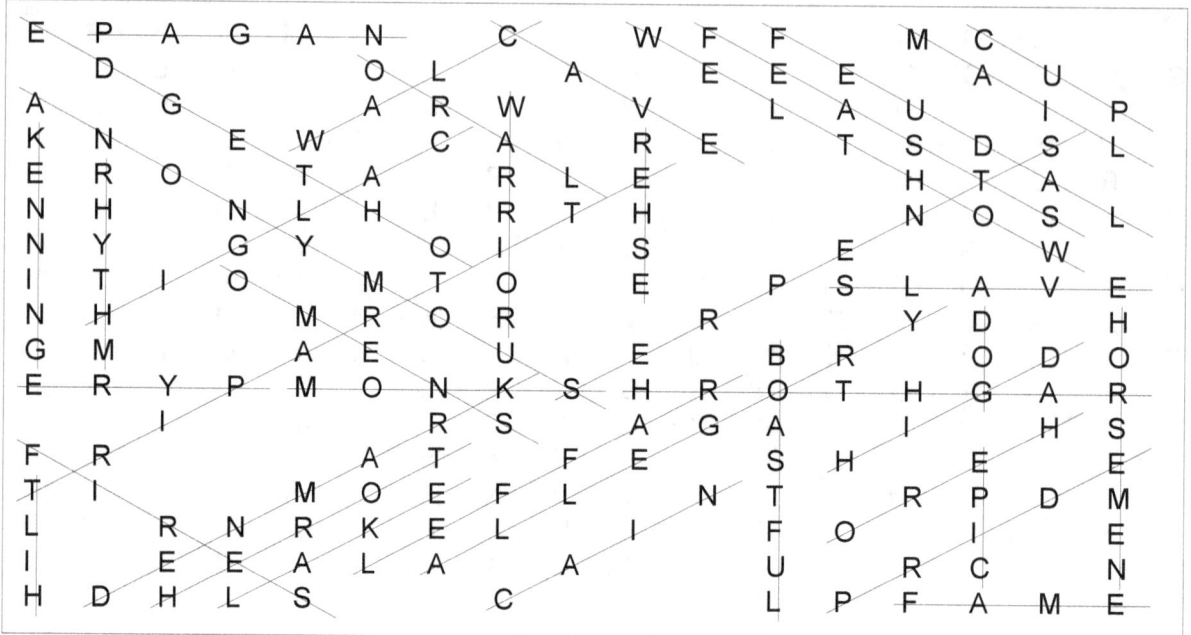

3-part story, such as Beowulf (10)
A story told on two levels (8)
Adjective that describes Unferth (8)
Anglo-Saxon metaphor (7)
Awakened the sleeping dragon (5)
Beowulf was first sung in this tradition (4)
Beowulf's father (7)
Beowulf's heathen origins (5)
Beowulf's inspiration (3)
Funeral fire (4)
Grendel and his mom live at the bottom of this (4)
Handle of a sword or dagger (4)
Higlac's wife (4)
Hrothgar's best friend; killed by Grendel's mother (5)
Hrothgar's homeland (7)
Hrothgar's mead hall (5)
Hrothgar's queen (7)
King of the Danes (8)
King of the Geats at the beginning of the epic (6)
Large parties that celebrate battle victories (6)
Lead characer of an epic; the protagonist (4)
Long, narrative poem (4)

Only part of Grendel left at Herot after the fight with Beowulf (4)
Person that Grendel and his mom were descended from (4)
Place where Grendel and his mother dwelled (4)
Protective chains worn by Beowulf (4)
Signs which predict the future (5)
Taken by slave from the dragon (3)
The Beowulf author (9)
The beat or cadence of the lines in poetry (6)
The only thing that lasts, according to the Anglo-Saxons (4)
They first put Beowulf in written form (5)
They rode around Beowulf's grave (8)
Times of the Anglo-Saxons (6)
Translator of Beowulf (6)
Type of person most prized in Anglo-Saxon society (7)
What Beowulf encountered and slew on the way to Grendel's mother (8)
What Hrothgar cautions Beowulf against (5)
What almost destroyed the last manuscript of Beowulf (5)

Beowulf Word Search 3

```
A L L I T E R A T I O N A I T S I R H C
N H F R G N T H Q M G J W T C W U S Q B
O R D W W D L Z W X O Y R E M I N G B K
N U G P K T C H V L H N G C C M F T Q Y
Y N W Z M X S V U A R L K A Y M E R S M
M T V D G F C F W R O P B S K I R I L G
O I B Y H Q T P B I T C Q U C N T P Z L
U N P M B S H Y G S H H Z R Q G H A S K
S G W M A T Y D X T G L M E D R C R S Y
N X D O H J W N G O A Z C V L B X T G T
F D B T K H G A Q C R M Z L R A K I P F
R N G S L N S L M D O Y A B R K T S J
Q U B F I H V T R A H H O R S E M E N N
W M V N M E X A W T P F K O M K R A E H
R G N R H R M E E I C D T J D P K M I E
H E R O T O W G C C L A W R E V A L S L
K I H W Y O D V O F A J I N N F T H N D
P S I Q H E M W W D L V T N M T E A E B
V L G T R F G Z A X H S E R A R F L M R
G W L C I P E F R R D I A B R C E L O W
M E A W E M A S D A R G C K U A E C M
W B C D B T E G S F F I Z D W P S G X J
J D I X G R Q Z A L N F O K C L T O X H
J R G L I X Y B U N J H E R Y P S R C P
P X G F W N B W F E U D A L B X K Y P F
```

ALLEGORY	EPIC	HORSEMEN	RHYTHM
ALLITERATION	ESHER	HROTHGAR	SERPENTS
ANONYMOUS	FAME	HRUNTING	SIEGMUND
ARISTOCRATIC	FEASTS	KENNING	SLAVE
BOASTFUL	FEUDAL	LAKE	SWIMMING
CAIN	FIRES	MAIL	TREASURE
CAVE	GEATLAND	MONKS	TRIPARTITE
CHRISTIAN	GOD	OMENS	UNFERTH
CLAW	HERO	ORAL	WARRIOR
COWARDS	HEROT	PAGAN	WELTHOW
CUP	HIGD	PRIDE	WULFGAR
DENMARK	HIGLAC	PYRE	
EDGETHO	HILT	RAFFEL	

Beowulf Word Search 3 Answer Key

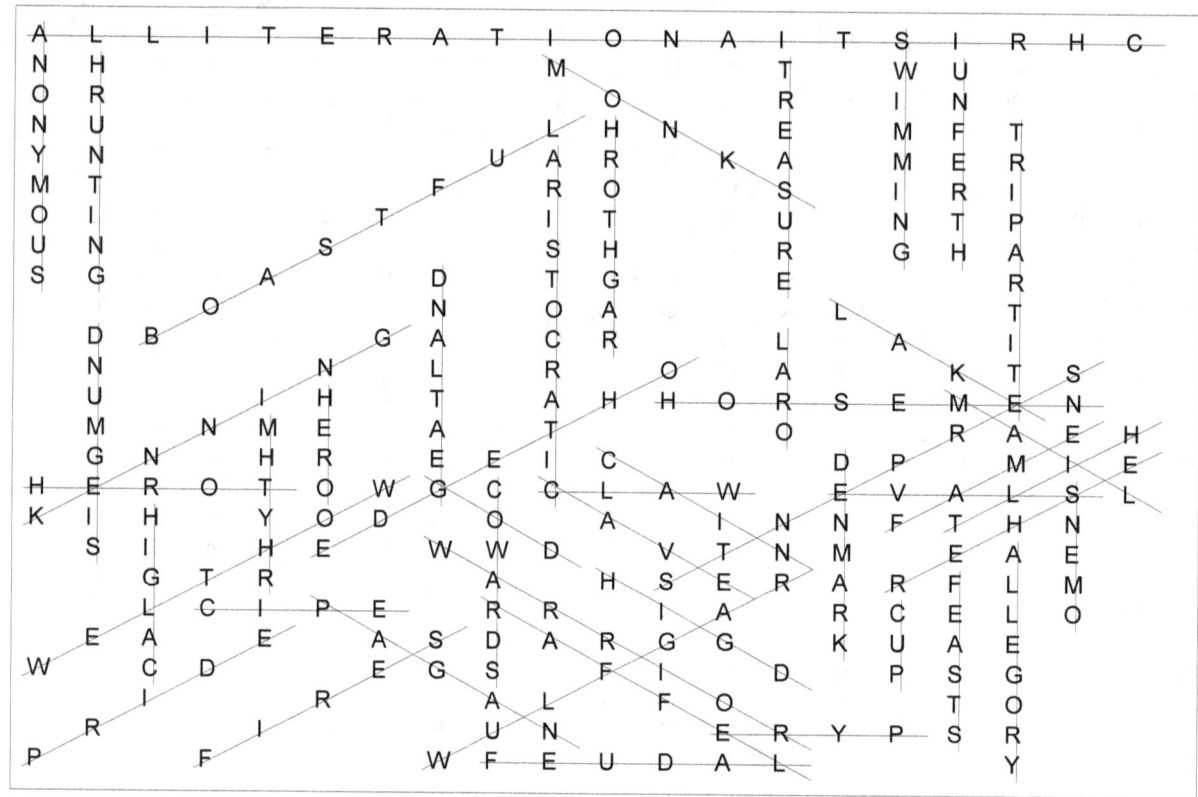

ALLEGORY	EPIC	HORSEMEN	RHYTHM
ALLITERATION	ESHER	HROTHGAR	SERPENTS
ANONYMOUS	FAME	HRUNTING	SIEGMUND
ARISTOCRATIC	FEASTS	KENNING	SLAVE
BOASTFUL	FEUDAL	LAKE	SWIMMING
CAIN	FIRES	MAIL	TREASURE
CAVE	GEATLAND	MONKS	TRIPARTITE
CHRISTIAN	GOD	OMENS	UNFERTH
CLAW	HERO	ORAL	WARRIOR
COWARDS	HEROT	PAGAN	WELTHOW
CUP	HIGD	PRIDE	WULFGAR
DENMARK	HIGLAC	PYRE	
EDGETHO	HILT	RAFFEL	

Beowulf Word Search 4

```
S W I M M I N G W U L F G A R S G D W T
H R N Q S T Y W N J R A N O N Y M O U S
R X A K T K Z J L W G J C H W M H D L N
U J R N F R S I E G M U N D R T Q W Z S
N W I H F S E T N S Z R G A L Q K A R X
T T S G U M N A P V V B G E G F P R H B
I R T H T N N D S J S H W R D I J R Y T
N H O V Z T F G S U T O G S W R N I T C
G P C E N R P E E O R R N E N E O H C
S L R C A I N Y R O G E L A S D R M F
K Y A I Y Q J H P T M H R V T I E A Z
P F T X D D P E E O H D W S X S L K T L
X S I Y T E V K N Q O D A Z T F B A B H
P U C G W A D N T G E E L I A M O L N X
B Z A A L H A L S N F Q A L W H A Z E D
W G L S R G I C M I G N L G T D S B M Y
E C G M A H Y A R N M I G E U P T X E Z
S H I P S M R P B N T H G E V S F H S F
H E H E L K O F X E C D F T D A U I R F
E R D P B M M N R K E R H R M R L G O N
R O W I M P P A K D C Q A E T A P D H V
H T J C J B T Q V S P W V W Z F L S X S
N C R P B I H N C C O A X V D F S Y Q J
P Z X C O N M G M C C X R M K E K G Z B
F J T N T R I P A R T I T E T L Y P X V
```

ALLEGORY
ALLITERATION
ANONYMOUS
ARISTOCRATIC
BOASTFUL
CAIN
CAVE
CHRISTIAN
CLAW
COWARDS
CUP
DENMARK
EDGETHO

EPIC
ESHER
FAME
FEASTS
FEUDAL
FIRES
GEATLAND
GOD
HERO
HEROT
HIGD
HIGLAC
HILT

HORSEMEN
HROTHGAR
HRUNTING
KENNING
LAKE
MAIL
MONKS
OMENS
ORAL
PAGAN
PRIDE
PYRE
RAFFEL

RHYTHM
SERPENTS
SIEGMUND
SLAVE
SWIMMING
TREASURE
TRIPARTITE
UNFERTH
WARRIOR
WELTHOW
WULFGAR

Beowulf Word Search 4 Answer Key

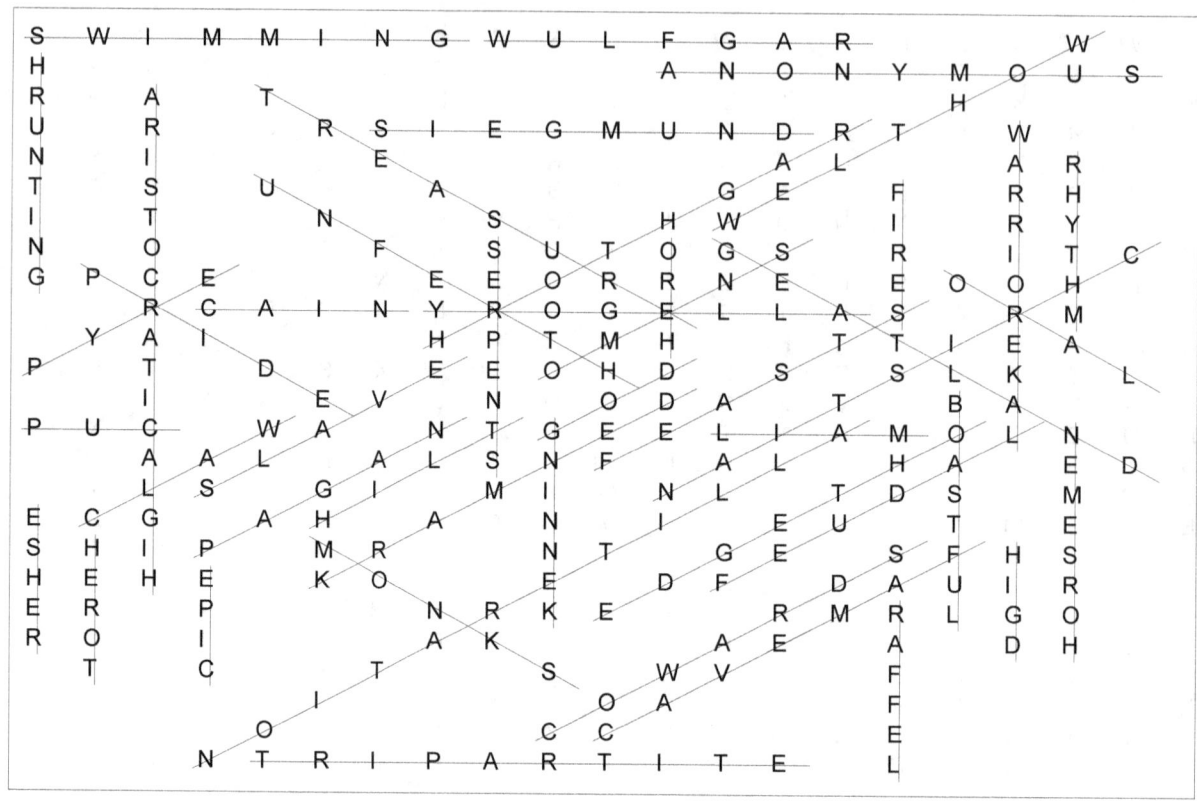

ALLEGORY	EPIC	HORSEMEN	RHYTHM
ALLITERATION	ESHER	HROTHGAR	SERPENTS
ANONYMOUS	FAME	HRUNTING	SIEGMUND
ARISTOCRATIC	FEASTS	KENNING	SLAVE
BOASTFUL	FEUDAL	LAKE	SWIMMING
CAIN	FIRES	MAIL	TREASURE
CAVE	GEATLAND	MONKS	TRIPARTITE
CHRISTIAN	GOD	OMENS	UNFERTH
CLAW	HERO	ORAL	WARRIOR
COWARDS	HEROT	PAGAN	WELTHOW
CUP	HIGD	PRIDE	WULFGAR
DENMARK	HIGLAC	PYRE	
EDGETHO	HILT	RAFFEL	

Beowulf Crossword 1

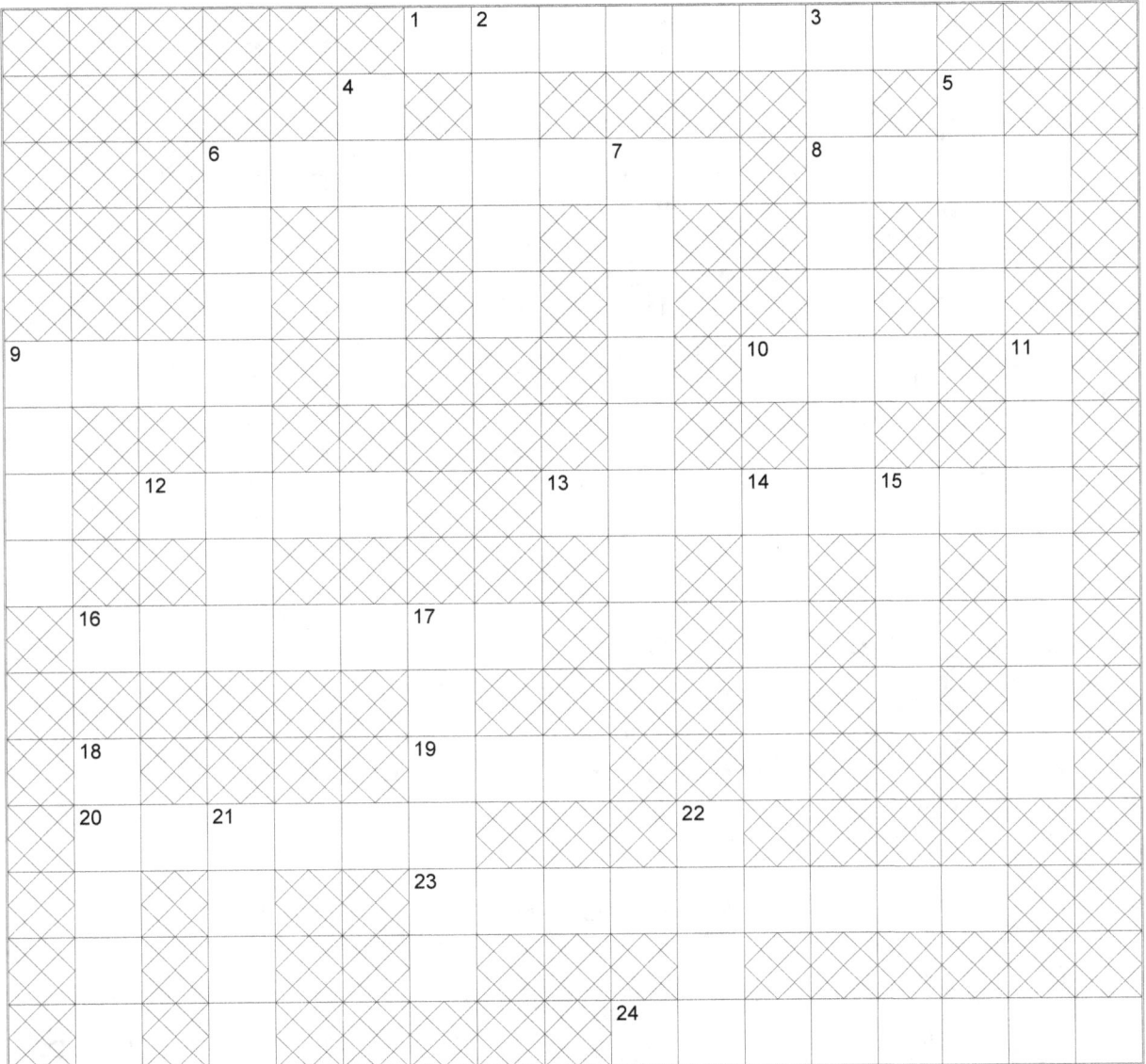

Across
1. What Beowulf encountered and slew on the way to Grendel's mother
6. King of the Danes
8. Long, narrative poem
9. Person that Grendel and his mom were descended from
10. Taken by slave from the dragon
12. Handle of a sword or dagger
13. They rode around Beowulf's grave
16. Beowulf's father
19. Beowulf's inspiration
20. Translator of Beowulf
23. The Beowulf author
24. Beowulf's homeland

Down
2. Hrothgar's best friend; killed by Grendel's mother
3. It was guarded by the dragon
4. They first put Beowulf in written form
5. Higlac's wife
6. Name of Unferth's sword
7. A story told on two levels
9. Place where Grendel and his mother dwelled
11. Hrothgar's homeland
14. Awakened the sleeping dragon
15. Protective chains worn by Beowulf
17. King of the Geats at the beginning of the epic
18. What Hrothgar cautions Beowulf against
21. The only thing that lasts, according to the Anglo-Saxons
22. Funeral fire

Beowulf Crossword 1 Answer Key

					¹S	²E	R	P	E	N	³T	S		
				⁴M		S					R		⁵H	
			⁶H	R	O	T	H	⁷G	A	R	⁸E	P	I	C
			R		N			E			A		G	
			U		K			R			S		D	
⁹C	A	I	N		S			E		¹⁰C	U	P	¹¹D	
A			T					G		R			E	
V		¹²H	I	L	T		¹³H	O	¹⁴R	S	¹⁵E	M	E	N
E		I					R		L		M		M	
	¹⁶E	D	G	E	T	¹⁷H	O		Y		A		I	A
						I					V		L	R
	¹⁸P			¹⁹G	O	D					E			K
	²⁰R	²¹A	F	F	E	L			²²P					
	I			²³A	N	O	N	Y	M	O	U	S		
	D		M		C				R					
	E		E				²⁴G	E	A	T	L	A	N	D

Across
1. What Beowulf encountered and slew on the way to Grendel's mother
6. King of the Danes
8. Long, narrative poem
9. Person that Grendel and his mom were descended from
10. Taken by slave from the dragon
12. Handle of a sword or dagger
13. They rode around Beowulf's grave
16. Beowulf's father
19. Beowulf's inspiration
20. Translator of Beowulf
23. The Beowulf author
24. Beowulf's homeland

Down
2. Hrothgar's best friend; killed by Grendel's mother
3. It was guarded by the dragon
4. They first put Beowulf in written form
5. Higlac's wife
6. Name of Unferth's sword
7. A story told on two levels
9. Place where Grendel and his mother dwelled
11. Hrothgar's homeland
14. Awakened the sleeping dragon
15. Protective chains worn by Beowulf
17. King of the Geats at the beginning of the epic
18. What Hrothgar cautions Beowulf against
21. The only thing that lasts, according to the Anglo-Saxons
22. Funeral fire

Beowulf Crossword 2

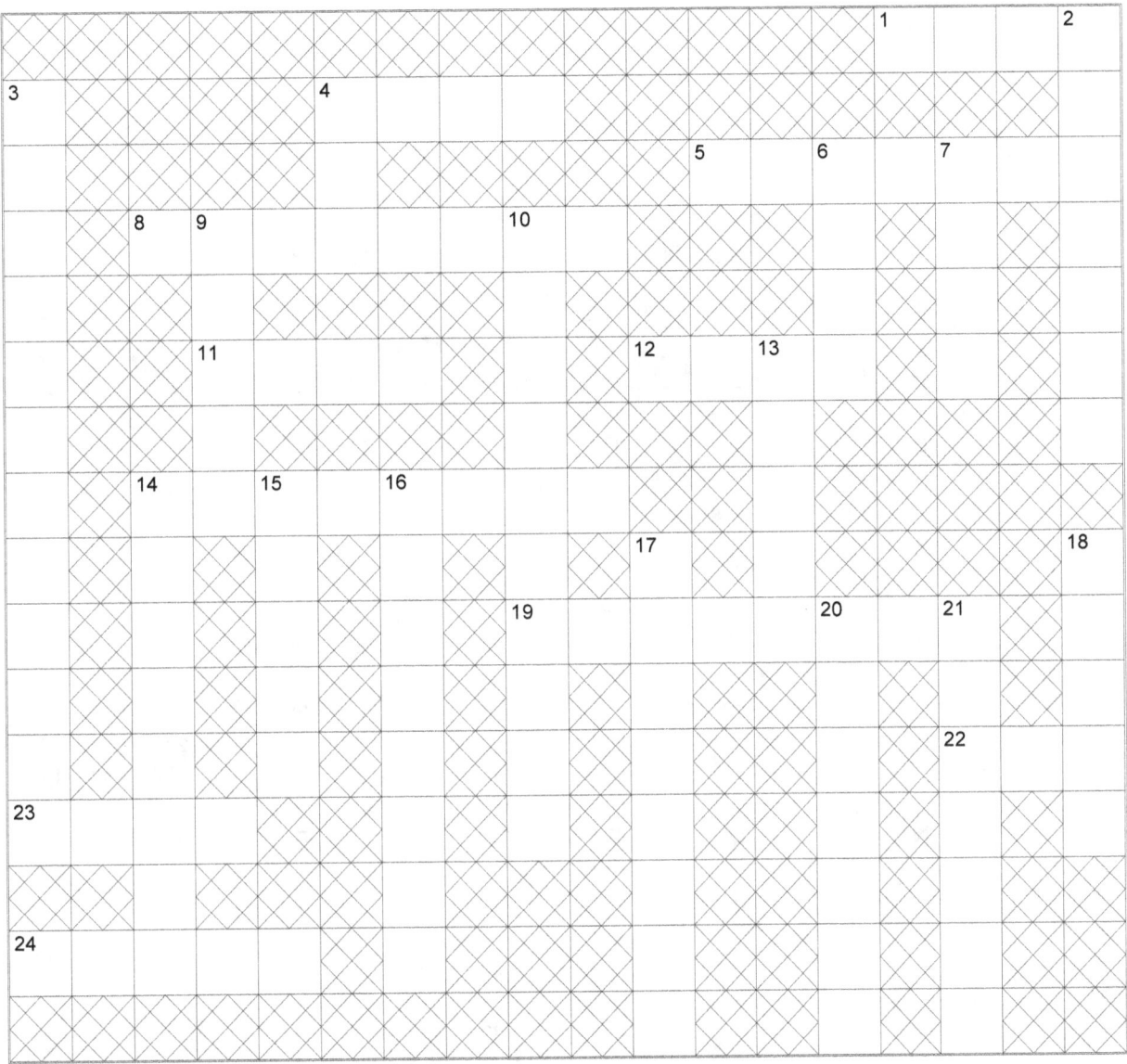

Across
1. Long, narrative poem
4. Place where Grendel and his mother dwelled
5. Hrothgar's queen
8. What Beowulf encountered and slew on the way to Grendel's mother
11. Higlac's wife
12. The only thing that lasts, according to the Anglo-Saxons
14. King of the Danes
19. It was guarded by the dragon
22. Beowulf's inspiration
23. Person that Grendel and his mom were descended from
24. Beowulf's heathen origins

Down
2. What Wiglaf calls Beowulf's soldiers
3. The Class of society that Beowulf is concerned with
4. Taken by slave from the dragon
6. Grendel and his mom live at the bottom of this
7. Handle of a sword or dagger
9. Hrothgar's best friend; killed by Grendel's mother
10. 3-part story, such as Beowulf
13. They first put Beowulf in written form
14. Name of Unferth's sword
15. Signs which predict the future
16. They rode around Beowulf's grave
17. Beowulf's homeland
18. What Hrothgar cautions Beowulf against
20. He challenged Beowulf's swimming prowess
21. Beowulf's father

Beowulf Crossword 2 Answer Key

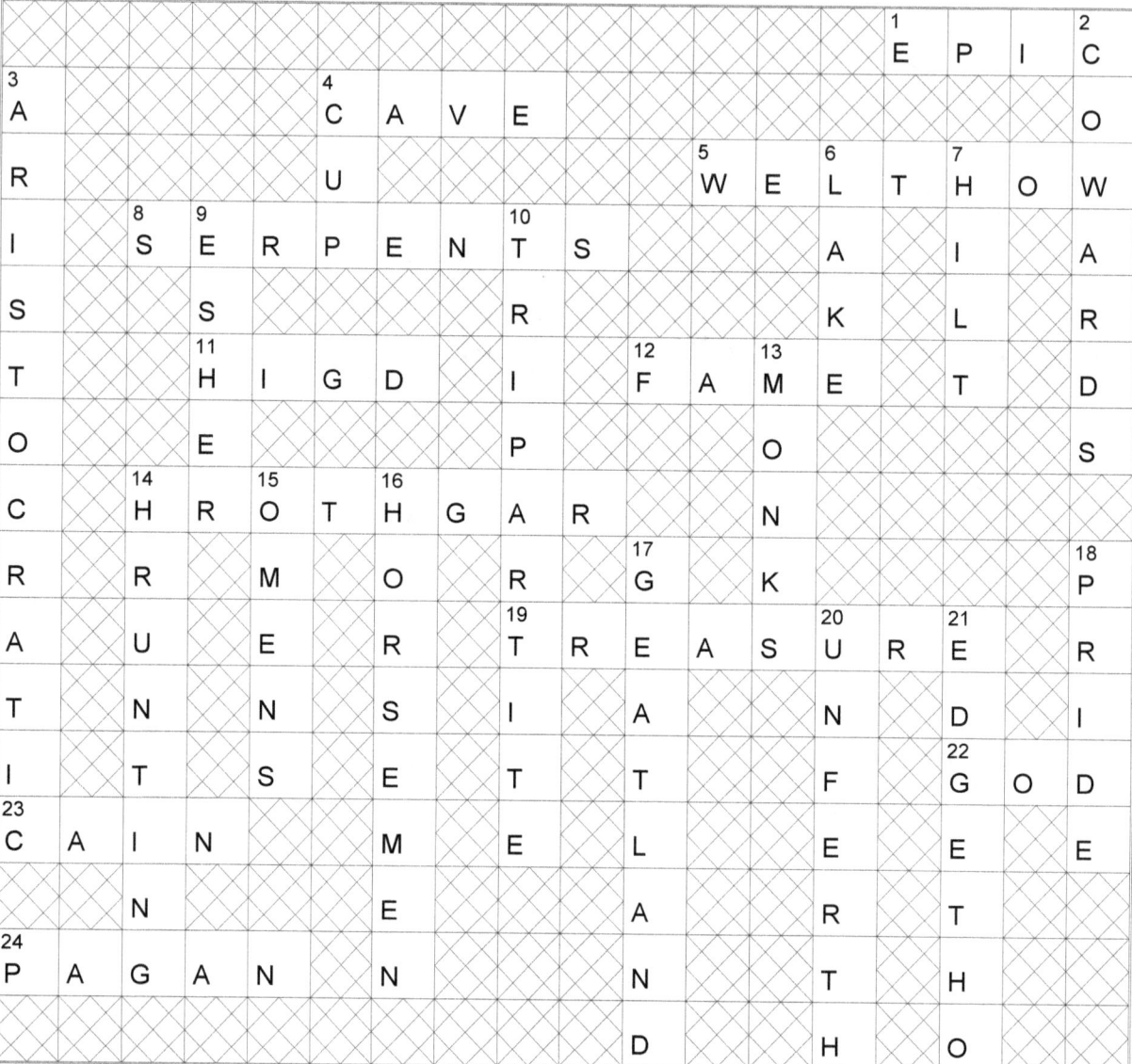

Across
1. Long, narrative poem
4. Place where Grendel and his mother dwelled
5. Hrothgar's queen
8. What Beowulf encountered and slew on the way to Grendel's mother
11. Higlac's wife
12. The only thing that lasts, according to the Anglo-Saxons
14. King of the Danes
19. It was guarded by the dragon
22. Beowulf's inspiration
23. Person that Grendel and his mom were descended from
24. Beowulf's heathen origins

Down
2. What Wiglaf calls Beowulf's soldiers
3. The Class of society that Beowulf is concerned with
4. Taken by slave from the dragon
6. Grendel and his mom live at the bottom of this
7. Handle of a sword or dagger
9. Hrothgar's best friend; killed by Grendel's mother
10. 3-part story, such as Beowulf
13. They first put Beowulf in written form
14. Name of Unferth's sword
15. Signs which predict the future
16. They rode around Beowulf's grave
17. Beowulf's homeland
18. What Hrothgar cautions Beowulf against
20. He challenged Beowulf's swimming prowess
21. Beowulf's father

Beowulf Crossword 3

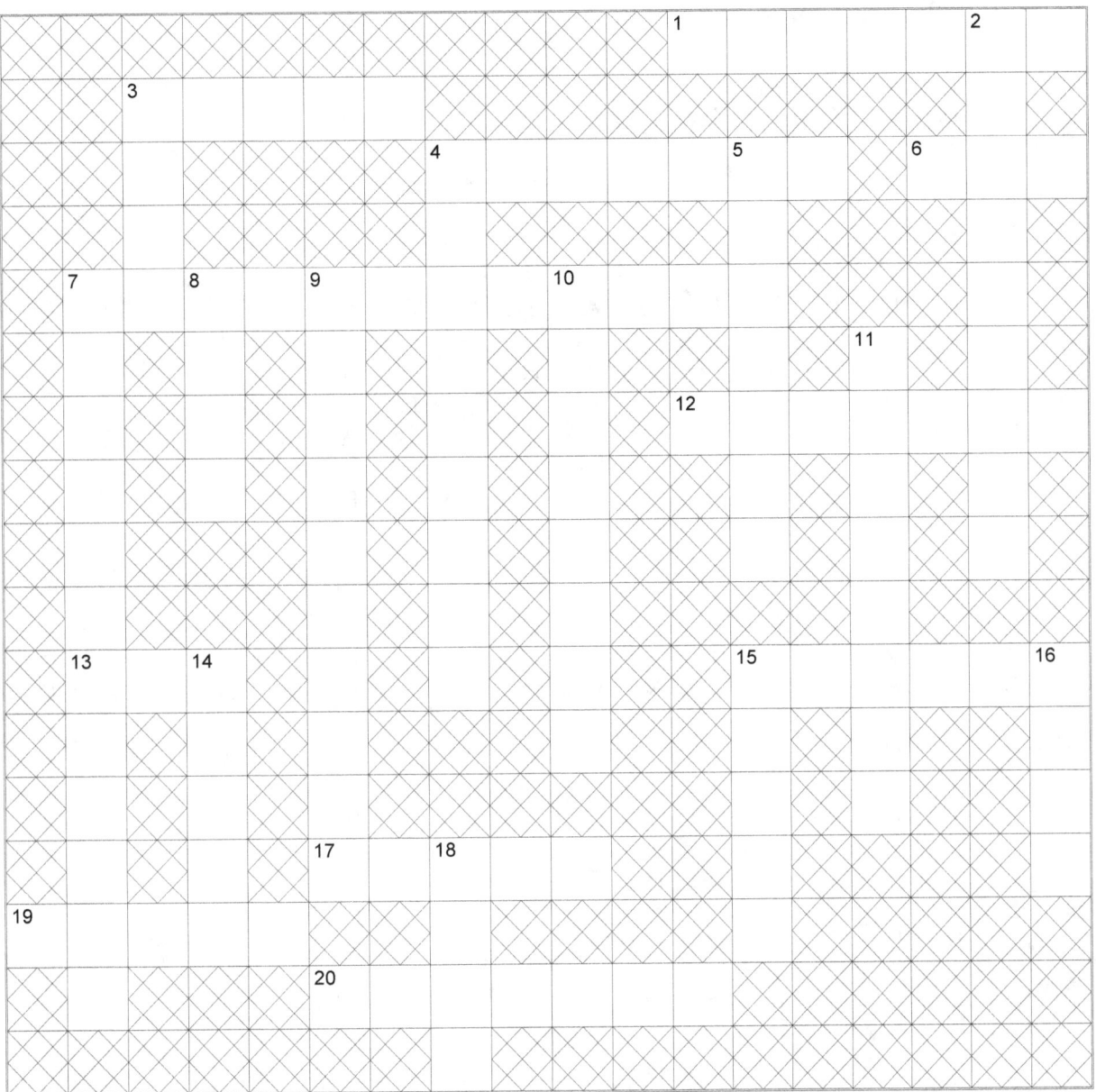

Across
1. Swedish prince who introduced Beowulf to Hrothgar
3. They first put Beowulf in written form
4. What Wiglaf calls Beowulf's soldiers
6. Beowulf's inspiration
7. Repetition of initial consonant sound
12. Type of person most prized in Anglo-Saxon society
13. Taken by slave from the dragon
15. King of the Geats at the beginning of the epic
17. Hrothgar's best friend; killed by Grendel's mother
19. What almost destroyed the last manuscript of Beowulf
20. Beowulf's father

Down
2. The Beowulf author
3. Protective chains worn by Beowulf
4. Influences that inserted God into this initially pagan text
5. Hrothgar's homeland
7. The Class of society that Beowulf is concerned with
8. Grendel and his mom live at the bottom of this
9. 3-part story, such as Beowulf
10. It was guarded by the dragon
11. King of the Danes
14. What Hrothgar cautions Beowulf against
15. Hrothgar's mead hall
16. Place where Grendel and his mother dwelled
18. Higlac's wife

Beowulf Crosword 3 Answer Key

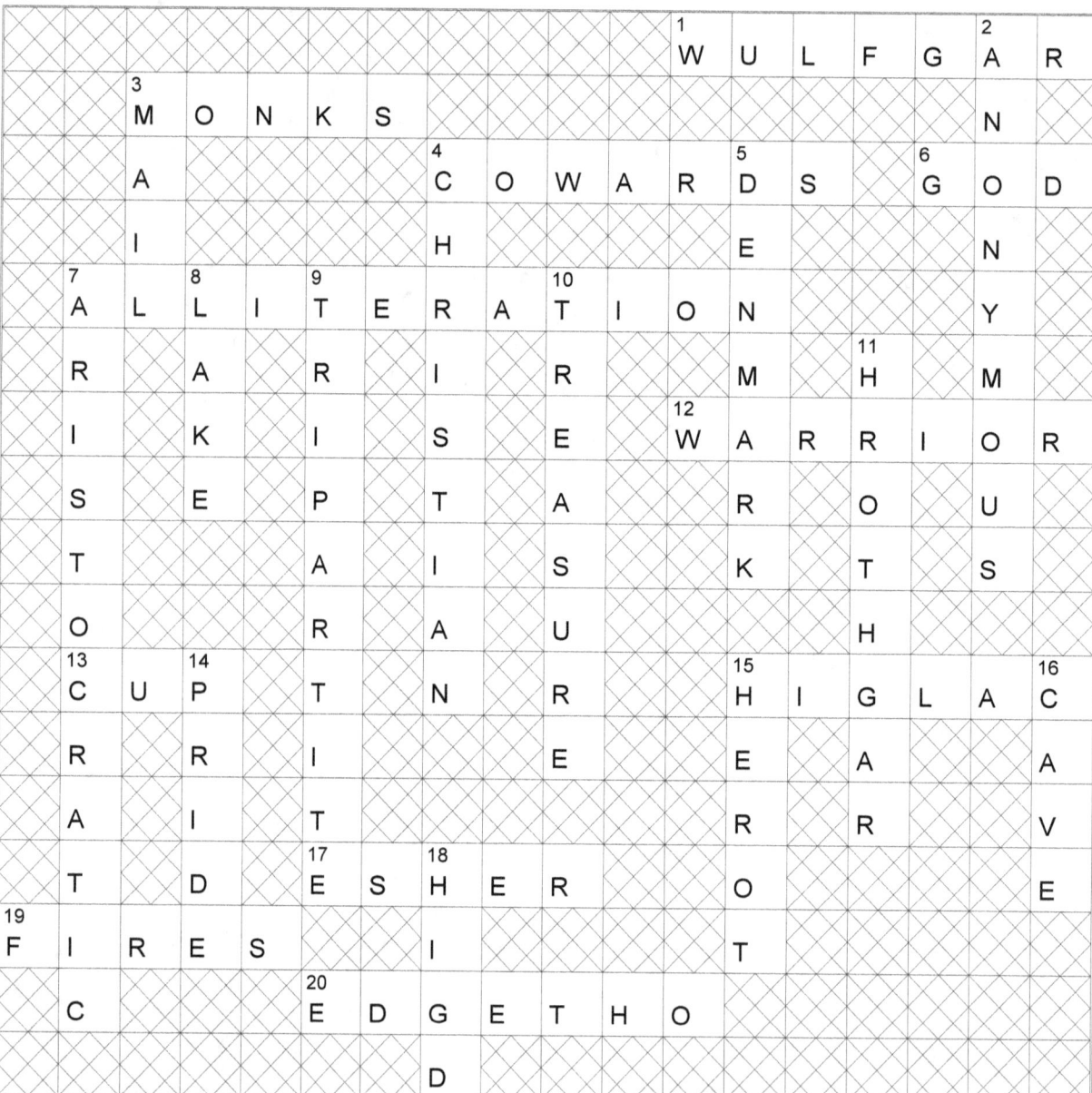

Across
1. Swedish prince who introduced Beowulf to Hrothgar
3. They first put Beowulf in written form
4. What Wiglaf calls Beowulf's soldiers
6. Beowulf's inspiration
7. Repetition of initial consonant sound
12. Type of person most prized in Anglo-Saxon society
13. Taken by slave from the dragon
15. King of the Geats at the beginning of the epic
17. Hrothgar's best friend; killed by Grendel's mother
19. What almost destroyed the last manuscript of Beowulf
20. Beowulf's father

Down
2. The Beowulf author
3. Protective chains worn by Beowulf
4. Influences that inserted God into this initially pagan text
5. Hrothgar's homeland
7. The Class of society that Beowulf is concerned with
8. Grendel and his mom live at the bottom of this
9. 3-part story, such as Beowulf
10. It was guarded by the dragon
11. King of the Danes
14. What Hrothgar cautions Beowulf against
15. Hrothgar's mead hall
16. Place where Grendel and his mother dwelled
18. Higlac's wife

Beowulf Crossword 4

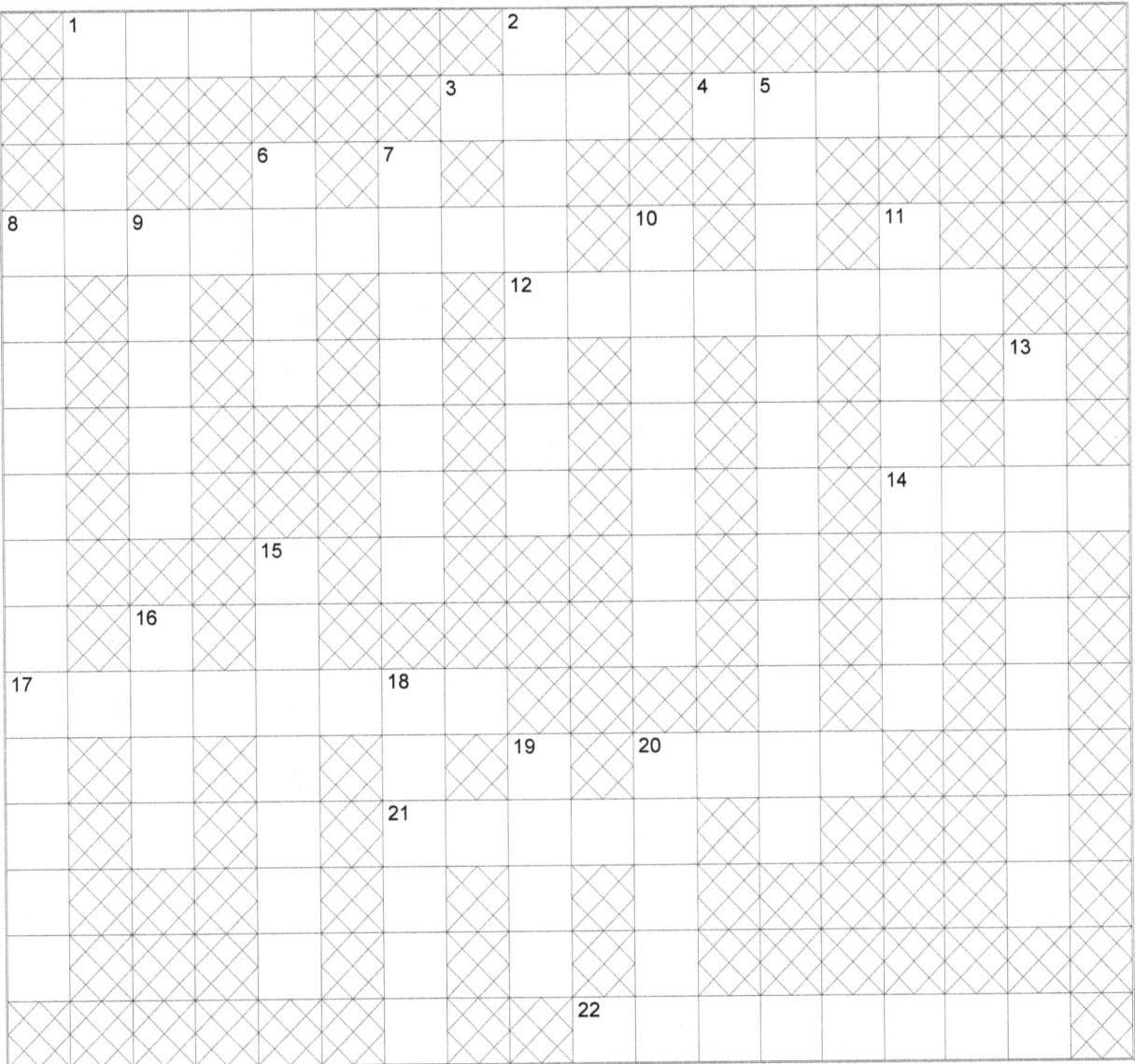

Across
1. Place where Grendel and his mother dwelled
3. Beowulf's inspiration
4. The only thing that lasts, according to the Anglo-Saxons
8. The Beowulf author
12. It was guarded by the dragon
14. Lead characer of an epic; the protagonist
17. A story told on two levels
20. Long, narrative poem
21. What almost destroyed the last manuscript of Beowulf
22. Name of Unferth's sword

Down
1. Person that Grendel and his mom were descended from
2. Adjective that describes Unferth
5. The Class of society that Beowulf is concerned with
6. Funeral fire
7. What Wiglaf calls Beowulf's soldiers
8. Repetition of initial consonant sound
9. Signs which predict the future
10. Hrothgar's homeland
11. King of the Danes
13. Influences that inserted God into this initially pagan text
15. Beowulf's father
16. Only part of Grendel left at Herot after the fight with Beowulf
18. Translator of Beowulf
19. Beowulf was first sung in this tradition
20. Hrothgar's best friend; killed by Grendel's mother

Beowulf Crossword 4 Answer Key

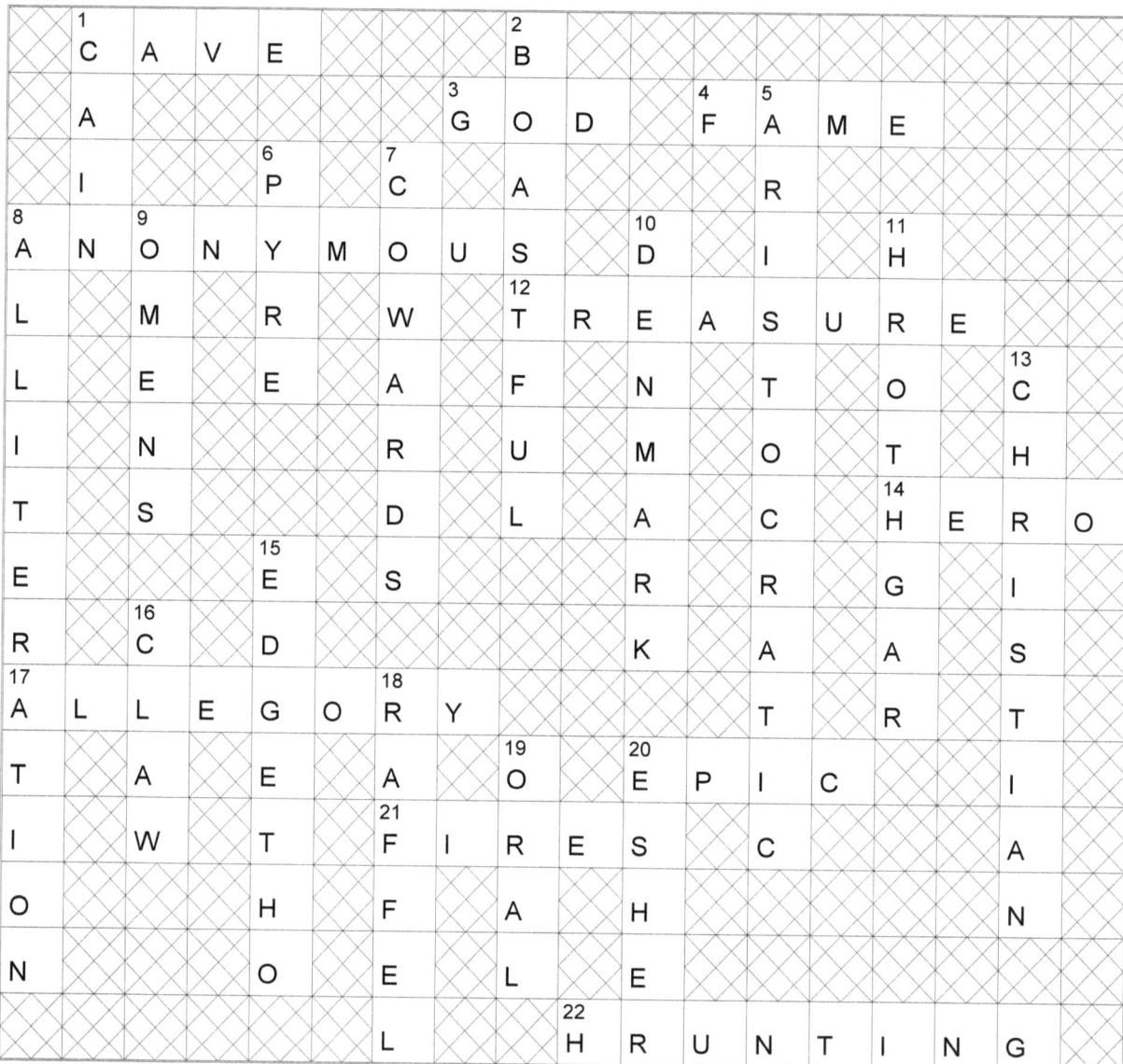

Across
1. Place where Grendel and his mother dwelled
3. Beowulf's inspiration
4. The only thing that lasts, according to the Anglo-Saxons
8. The Beowulf author
12. It was guarded by the dragon
14. Lead characer of an epic; the protagonist
17. A story told on two levels
20. Long, narrative poem
21. What almost destroyed the last manuscript of Beowulf
22. Name of Unferth's sword

Down
1. Person that Grendel and his mom were descended from
2. Adjective that describes Unferth
5. The Class of society that Beowulf is concerned with
6. Funeral fire
7. What Wiglaf calls Beowulf's soldiers
8. Repetition of initial consonant sound
9. Signs which predict the future
10. Hrothgar's homeland
11. King of the Danes
13. Influences that inserted God into this initially pagan text
15. Beowulf's father
16. Only part of Grendel left at Herot after the fight with Beowulf
18. Translator of Beowulf
19. Beowulf was first sung in this tradition
20. Hrothgar's best friend; killed by Grendel's mother

Beowulf

SIEGMUND	UNFERTH	FEUDAL	CAIN	SERPENTS
SLAVE	PYRE	ORAL	KENNING	WELTHOW
EPIC	FIRES	FREE SPACE	OMENS	BOASTFUL
HRUNTING	LAKE	ESHER	HEROT	WULFGAR
CLAW	CAVE	PAGAN	GOD	TREASURE

Beowulf

ARISTOCRATIC	COWARDS	TRIPARTITE	HIGD	HILT
DENMARK	ALLITERATION	EDGETHO	FEASTS	MONKS
RAFFEL	PRIDE	FREE SPACE	GEATLAND	SWIMMING
HROTHGAR	CHRISTIAN	CUP	HIGLAC	FAME
RHYTHM	HORSEMEN	WARRIOR	ALLEGORY	ANONYMOUS

Beowulf

HERO	HILT	MAIL	CUP	WELTHOW
ESHER	FEUDAL	CAIN	GEATLAND	FAME
HEROT	KENNING	FREE SPACE	SIEGMUND	HIGD
ARISTOCRATIC	ALLEGORY	PYRE	HRUNTING	ORAL
ALLITERATION	HIGLAC	CAVE	CHRISTIAN	GOD

Beowulf

PAGAN	OMENS	SERPENTS	WARRIOR	CLAW
UNFERTH	TRIPARTITE	WULFGAR	SLAVE	FIRES
SWIMMING	HROTHGAR	FREE SPACE	TREASURE	PRIDE
COWARDS	EPIC	FEASTS	ANONYMOUS	LAKE
BOASTFUL	RAFFEL	EDGETHO	RHYTHM	DENMARK

Beowulf

CLAW	HEROT	GOD	CAVE	OMENS
FEUDAL	WULFGAR	PYRE	FIRES	HIGD
FAME	MONKS	FREE SPACE	PRIDE	HILT
RHYTHM	WELTHOW	HROTHGAR	KENNING	ANONYMOUS
PAGAN	CAIN	COWARDS	TREASURE	DENMARK

Beowulf

CHRISTIAN	ORAL	FEASTS	WARRIOR	RAFFEL
SERPENTS	EPIC	UNFERTH	EDGETHO	TRIPARTITE
HERO	HIGLAC	FREE SPACE	CUP	HORSEMEN
GEATLAND	SIEGMUND	HRUNTING	ARISTOCRATIC	ALLITERATION
ESHER	SWIMMING	ALLEGORY	BOASTFUL	MAIL

Beowulf

WULFGAR	UNFERTH	HRUNTING	SERPENTS	TREASURE
RAFFEL	WELTHOW	COWARDS	EPIC	TRIPARTITE
HILT	RHYTHM	FREE SPACE	GEATLAND	HERO
CUP	OMENS	CHRISTIAN	HIGD	CAVE
ALLEGORY	FEUDAL	HEROT	MONKS	ESHER

Beowulf

LAKE	PRIDE	SWIMMING	ALLITERATION	WARRIOR
HROTHGAR	FAME	CLAW	PYRE	FIRES
HORSEMEN	GOD	FREE SPACE	ORAL	FEASTS
EDGETHO	HIGLAC	CAIN	DENMARK	SLAVE
BOASTFUL	PAGAN	MAIL	ANONYMOUS	SIEGMUND

Beowulf

SERPENTS	TRIPARTITE	FEASTS	WULFGAR	MONKS
CUP	HEROT	ALLEGORY	PAGAN	ANONYMOUS
MAIL	LAKE	FREE SPACE	DENMARK	KENNING
SWIMMING	BOASTFUL	HILT	FIRES	GOD
CAIN	UNFERTH	RHYTHM	RAFFEL	WELTHOW

Beowulf

CHRISTIAN	EDGETHO	HROTHGAR	CAVE	ORAL
HERO	SIEGMUND	ESHER	PRIDE	FAME
HIGD	GEATLAND	FREE SPACE	COWARDS	ALLITERATION
SLAVE	ARISTOCRATIC	OMENS	TREASURE	EPIC
CLAW	HORSEMEN	HRUNTING	PYRE	HIGLAC

Beowulf

CLAW	TRIPARTITE	MAIL	SIEGMUND	GOD
MONKS	CUP	WARRIOR	CAIN	BOASTFUL
HORSEMEN	HRUNTING	FREE SPACE	PRIDE	PAGAN
RHYTHM	SLAVE	EDGETHO	EPIC	COWARDS
GEATLAND	SWIMMING	HEROT	HERO	ARISTOCRATIC

Beowulf

HIGD	HIGLAC	HROTHGAR	HILT	CHRISTIAN
FAME	PYRE	CAVE	LAKE	WULFGAR
UNFERTH	ALLITERATION	FREE SPACE	ANONYMOUS	ALLEGORY
WELTHOW	RAFFEL	ORAL	FIRES	FEASTS
OMENS	SERPENTS	TREASURE	ESHER	FEUDAL

Beowulf

TREASURE	OMENS	LAKE	CAIN	SWIMMING
HIGLAC	GOD	CUP	RHYTHM	ESHER
HERO	ALLITERATION	FREE SPACE	KENNING	DENMARK
PYRE	RAFFEL	FAME	HORSEMEN	FEUDAL
HEROT	COWARDS	TRIPARTITE	SIEGMUND	EDGETHO

Beowulf

WARRIOR	HIGD	SLAVE	FEASTS	FIRES
GEATLAND	BOASTFUL	CHRISTIAN	UNFERTH	CAVE
ALLEGORY	HILT	FREE SPACE	MONKS	WELTHOW
HROTHGAR	HRUNTING	ORAL	MAIL	SERPENTS
EPIC	WULFGAR	PAGAN	PRIDE	CLAW

Beowulf

CAIN	GEATLAND	FAME	LAKE	FEASTS
SERPENTS	ORAL	CLAW	PYRE	RAFFEL
TREASURE	COWARDS	FREE SPACE	HRUNTING	SWIMMING
RHYTHM	UNFERTH	WELTHOW	CUP	ALLITERATION
HILT	HIGLAC	DENMARK	HIGD	FIRES

Beowulf

ARISTOCRATIC	HERO	EPIC	WARRIOR	GOD
CHRISTIAN	MAIL	CAVE	MONKS	HROTHGAR
SLAVE	ALLEGORY	FREE SPACE	PAGAN	ESHER
SIEGMUND	HORSEMEN	FEUDAL	HEROT	WULFGAR
OMENS	BOASTFUL	ANONYMOUS	TRIPARTITE	EDGETHO

Beowulf

ORAL	LAKE	ALLITERATION	PYRE	CAVE
ARISTOCRATIC	CUP	SWIMMING	MAIL	PRIDE
WULFGAR	GOD	FREE SPACE	SLAVE	HRUNTING
EDGETHO	ANONYMOUS	SERPENTS	COWARDS	GEATLAND
FEUDAL	ESHER	HIGLAC	HILT	RHYTHM

Beowulf

PAGAN	MONKS	KENNING	EPIC	HORSEMEN
OMENS	RAFFEL	UNFERTH	HIGD	CLAW
FEASTS	WELTHOW	FREE SPACE	ALLEGORY	TREASURE
CHRISTIAN	HEROT	WARRIOR	DENMARK	FIRES
FAME	HERO	CAIN	HROTHGAR	SIEGMUND

Beowulf

FEASTS	SIEGMUND	DENMARK	HIGD	PYRE
PRIDE	CAIN	COWARDS	KENNING	RAFFEL
ANONYMOUS	RHYTHM	FREE SPACE	HEROT	ALLEGORY
FEUDAL	WELTHOW	EPIC	PAGAN	BOASTFUL
HERO	HIGLAC	HROTHGAR	FAME	HRUNTING

Beowulf

CLAW	ESHER	ALLITERATION	EDGETHO	MAIL
SWIMMING	SERPENTS	FIRES	HILT	GOD
UNFERTH	TREASURE	FREE SPACE	MONKS	SLAVE
CHRISTIAN	CAVE	HORSEMEN	ORAL	OMENS
LAKE	CUP	TRIPARTITE	WULFGAR	GEATLAND

Beowulf

PRIDE	EPIC	CAIN	TRIPARTITE	BOASTFUL
MAIL	ANONYMOUS	RAFFEL	ORAL	HORSEMEN
DENMARK	WELTHOW	FREE SPACE	LAKE	CLAW
HRUNTING	SLAVE	ALLITERATION	TREASURE	SERPENTS
HILT	FEASTS	OMENS	UNFERTH	HERO

Beowulf

WULFGAR	HEROT	ALLEGORY	HROTHGAR	KENNING
HIGD	FAME	GOD	HIGLAC	PYRE
SIEGMUND	FEUDAL	FREE SPACE	SWIMMING	ARISTOCRATIC
CHRISTIAN	GEATLAND	FIRES	MONKS	RHYTHM
PAGAN	EDGETHO	COWARDS	WARRIOR	CUP

Beowulf

CLAW	FIRES	EDGETHO	ALLITERATION	DENMARK
WARRIOR	WULFGAR	HRUNTING	SERPENTS	SWIMMING
CHRISTIAN	FAME	FREE SPACE	BOASTFUL	TREASURE
ARISTOCRATIC	PAGAN	PRIDE	EPIC	CAVE
CAIN	HIGLAC	HILT	HROTHGAR	FEASTS

Beowulf

COWARDS	MONKS	OMENS	GEATLAND	RHYTHM
KENNING	ORAL	WELTHOW	HORSEMEN	GOD
CUP	RAFFEL	FREE SPACE	SLAVE	UNFERTH
ESHER	HIGD	MAIL	FEUDAL	LAKE
HEROT	ALLEGORY	PYRE	TRIPARTITE	SIEGMUND

Beowulf

CAIN	CUP	HORSEMEN	SERPENTS	SLAVE
ORAL	DENMARK	RAFFEL	WELTHOW	PAGAN
ARISTOCRATIC	FIRES	FREE SPACE	TRIPARTITE	PYRE
CHRISTIAN	TREASURE	EDGETHO	HEROT	CLAW
ALLEGORY	ANONYMOUS	RHYTHM	SWIMMING	HILT

Beowulf

OMENS	FAME	WARRIOR	GEATLAND	CAVE
ALLITERATION	EPIC	HIGD	HROTHGAR	ESHER
HIGLAC	FEUDAL	FREE SPACE	WULFGAR	LAKE
UNFERTH	HERO	FEASTS	PRIDE	MAIL
SIEGMUND	GOD	MONKS	COWARDS	BOASTFUL

Beowulf

BOASTFUL	EDGETHO	FEUDAL	CAVE	LAKE
HORSEMEN	CUP	ALLEGORY	COWARDS	GEATLAND
GOD	TREASURE	FREE SPACE	OMENS	HROTHGAR
MAIL	PYRE	WELTHOW	EPIC	ESHER
CAIN	SERPENTS	RAFFEL	ALLITERATION	HERO

Beowulf

HIGD	PAGAN	ANONYMOUS	FIRES	ARISTOCRATIC
CHRISTIAN	SLAVE	DENMARK	HILT	SIEGMUND
TRIPARTITE	ORAL	FREE SPACE	WARRIOR	FAME
KENNING	RHYTHM	CLAW	WULFGAR	UNFERTH
MONKS	PRIDE	HRUNTING	FEASTS	SWIMMING

Beowulf

HIGLAC	HEROT	SIEGMUND	GOD	CAVE
RHYTHM	HILT	ALLITERATION	COWARDS	MONKS
PYRE	SWIMMING	FREE SPACE	WELTHOW	ALLEGORY
TREASURE	CUP	KENNING	PAGAN	FIRES
CAIN	HORSEMEN	RAFFEL	PRIDE	OMENS

Beowulf

LAKE	FEUDAL	BOASTFUL	HRUNTING	TRIPARTITE
SERPENTS	ANONYMOUS	ESHER	ARISTOCRATIC	FAME
EPIC	WARRIOR	FREE SPACE	CHRISTIAN	EDGETHO
HIGD	FEASTS	WULFGAR	HROTHGAR	SLAVE
MAIL	DENMARK	HERO	CLAW	UNFERTH

Beowulf

OMENS	UNFERTH	MONKS	SIEGMUND	WELTHOW
DENMARK	ALLEGORY	CHRISTIAN	SERPENTS	HIGLAC
HORSEMEN	WULFGAR	FREE SPACE	HERO	ESHER
ARISTOCRATIC	FAME	RAFFEL	KENNING	PAGAN
PYRE	SWIMMING	ORAL	LAKE	RHYTHM

Beowulf

GOD	PRIDE	HROTHGAR	CAIN	MAIL
EDGETHO	SLAVE	COWARDS	ALLITERATION	EPIC
CUP	ANONYMOUS	FREE SPACE	CAVE	GEATLAND
FEUDAL	CLAW	HIGD	WARRIOR	FEASTS
FIRES	TRIPARTITE	HILT	HEROT	BOASTFUL

Beowulf Vocabulary Word List

No.	Word	Clue/Definition
1.	ASCRIBED	Attributed; assigned
2.	BELCHING	Bursting with flame or smoke
3.	BILLOWING	Flowing; rising on the winds
4.	CHARRING	Burning
5.	COBBLED	Stones roughly placed together
6.	COMPELLED	Forced
7.	DECREED	Ordered by a judge
8.	DISSOLUTION	Dispersal
9.	EARTHEN	Made of dirt
10.	ELUCIDATE	Make clear
11.	EMULATED	Rival with some degree of success
12.	EXULTING	Rejoicing triumphantly
13.	FURROWS	Narrow, trench-like depressions
14.	GROPED	Searched for blindly
15.	HAG	Repulsive old woman
16.	HALTINGLY	With hesitation
17.	HEATHEN	Pagan; non-Christian
18.	HILT	Handle of a sword or dagger
19.	HOARDS	A group or accumulation
20.	JACKAL	One who meanly serves the purpose of another
21.	LINDEN	Trees with heart-shaped leaves
22.	MALICE	Evil intent
23.	NIGGARDLY	Stingy
24.	OMENS	Signs of things to come
25.	PYRE	Pile of wood for burning dead bodies
26.	REPARATION	Process of making amends
27.	REPRISAL	Retaliation; revenge
28.	RUMINATIVE	Meditative; pondering
29.	RUNIC	Ancient, interlacing script
30.	SCABBARD	Sheath or cover for a sword
31.	SOLACE	Comfort in sorrow
32.	SOLICITUDE	Anxiety or concern
33.	TALONS	Claws
34.	TARNISH	Discoloration of metal
35.	TAUT	Tight
36.	TRIPARTITE	Consisting of three parts
37.	UNAIDED	Without help
38.	VENOM	Poison
39.	WRETCHED	Miserable; pitiable
40.	WRITHING	Twisting and squirming

Beowulf Vocabulary Fill In The Blank 1

1. Tight
2. Forced
3. Retaliation; revenge
4. Repulsive old woman
5. Comfort in sorrow
6. Pile of wood for burning dead bodies
7. Process of making amends
8. Poison
9. Narrow, trench-like depressions
10. Stingy
11. Flowing; rising on the winds
12. Ancient, interlacing script
13. Searched for blindly
14. Burning
15. Sheath or cover for a sword
16. With hesitation
17. Dispersal
18. Rival with some degree of success
19. Pagan; non-Christian
20. One who meanly serves the purpose of another

Beowulf Vocabulary Fill In The Blank 1 Answer Key

TAUT	1. Tight
COMPELLED	2. Forced
REPRISAL	3. Retaliation; revenge
HAG	4. Repulsive old woman
SOLACE	5. Comfort in sorrow
PYRE	6. Pile of wood for burning dead bodies
REPARATION	7. Process of making amends
VENOM	8. Poison
FURROWS	9. Narrow, trench-like depressions
NIGGARDLY	10. Stingy
BILLOWING	11. Flowing; rising on the winds
RUNIC	12. Ancient, interlacing script
GROPED	13. Searched for blindly
CHARRING	14. Burning
SCABBARD	15. Sheath or cover for a sword
HALTINGLY	16. With hesitation
DISSOLUTION	17. Dispersal
EMULATED	18. Rival with some degree of success
HEATHEN	19. Pagan; non-Christian
JACKAL	20. One who meanly serves the purpose of another

Beowulf Vocabulary Fill In The Blank 2

_____ 1. Ancient, interlacing script

_____ 2. Poison

_____ 3. Burning

_____ 4. Process of making amends

_____ 5. Ordered by a judge

_____ 6. Signs of things to come

_____ 7. One who meanly serves the purpose of another

_____ 8. Made of dirt

_____ 9. Repulsive old woman

_____ 10. Meditative; pondering

_____ 11. Comfort in sorrow

_____ 12. Anxiety or concern

_____ 13. Pagan; non-Christian

_____ 14. Bursting with flame or smoke

_____ 15. Attributed; assigned

_____ 16. Narrow, trench-like depressions

_____ 17. Handle of a sword or dagger

_____ 18. Miserable; pitiable

_____ 19. Rejoicing triumphantly

_____ 20. Consisting of three parts

Beowulf Vocabulary Fill In The Blank 2 Answer Key

RUNIC	1. Ancient, interlacing script
VENOM	2. Poison
CHARRING	3. Burning
REPARATION	4. Process of making amends
DECREED	5. Ordered by a judge
OMENS	6. Signs of things to come
JACKAL	7. One who meanly serves the purpose of another
EARTHEN	8. Made of dirt
HAG	9. Repulsive old woman
RUMINATIVE	10. Meditative; pondering
SOLACE	11. Comfort in sorrow
SOLICITUDE	12. Anxiety or concern
HEATHEN	13. Pagan; non-Christian
BELCHING	14. Bursting with flame or smoke
ASCRIBED	15. Attributed; assigned
FURROWS	16. Narrow, trench-like depressions
HILT	17. Handle of a sword or dagger
WRETCHED	18. Miserable; pitiable
EXULTING	19. Rejoicing triumphantly
TRIPARTITE	20. Consisting of three parts

Beowulf Vocabulary Fill In The Blank 3

_____ 1. Sheath or cover for a sword

_____ 2. Pile of wood for burning dead bodies

_____ 3. Made of dirt

_____ 4. Stingy

_____ 5. Process of making amends

_____ 6. Comfort in sorrow

_____ 7. Repulsive old woman

_____ 8. Evil intent

_____ 9. A group or accumulation

_____ 10. Ordered by a judge

_____ 11. Burning

_____ 12. Discoloration of metal

_____ 13. Tight

_____ 14. With hesitation

_____ 15. Make clear

_____ 16. Flowing; rising on the winds

_____ 17. Stones roughly placed together

_____ 18. Trees with heart-shaped leaves

_____ 19. Anxiety or concern

_____ 20. Poison

Beowulf Vocabulary Fill In The Blank 3 Answer Key

SCABBARD	1. Sheath or cover for a sword
PYRE	2. Pile of wood for burning dead bodies
EARTHEN	3. Made of dirt
NIGGARDLY	4. Stingy
REPARATION	5. Process of making amends
SOLACE	6. Comfort in sorrow
HAG	7. Repulsive old woman
MALICE	8. Evil intent
HOARDS	9. A group or accumulation
DECREED	10. Ordered by a judge
CHARRING	11. Burning
TARNISH	12. Discoloration of metal
TAUT	13. Tight
HALTINGLY	14. With hesitation
ELUCIDATE	15. Make clear
BILLOWING	16. Flowing; rising on the winds
COBBLED	17. Stones roughly placed together
LINDEN	18. Trees with heart-shaped leaves
SOLICITUDE	19. Anxiety or concern
VENOM	20. Poison

Beowulf Vocabulary Fill In The Blank 4

_____ 1. Repulsive old woman

_____ 2. Burning

_____ 3. One who meanly serves the purpose of another

_____ 4. Stingy

_____ 5. Ordered by a judge

_____ 6. Stones roughly placed together

_____ 7. A group or accumulation

_____ 8. Pagan; non-Christian

_____ 9. Bursting with flame or smoke

_____ 10. Without help

_____ 11. Evil intent

_____ 12. Twisting and squirming

_____ 13. Rejoicing triumphantly

_____ 14. Meditative; pondering

_____ 15. Handle of a sword or dagger

_____ 16. Forced

_____ 17. Flowing; rising on the winds

_____ 18. Retaliation; revenge

_____ 19. Dispersal

_____ 20. Signs of things to come

Beowulf Vocabulary Fill In The Blank 4 Answer Key

HAG	1. Repulsive old woman
CHARRING	2. Burning
JACKAL	3. One who meanly serves the purpose of another
NIGGARDLY	4. Stingy
DECREED	5. Ordered by a judge
COBBLED	6. Stones roughly placed together
HOARDS	7. A group or accumulation
HEATHEN	8. Pagan; non-Christian
BELCHING	9. Bursting with flame or smoke
UNAIDED	10. Without help
MALICE	11. Evil intent
WRITHING	12. Twisting and squirming
EXULTING	13. Rejoicing triumphantly
RUMINATIVE	14. Meditative; pondering
HILT	15. Handle of a sword or dagger
COMPELLED	16. Forced
BILLOWING	17. Flowing; rising on the winds
REPRISAL	18. Retaliation; revenge
DISSOLUTION	19. Dispersal
OMENS	20. Signs of things to come

Beowulf Vocabulary Matching 1

___ 1. COMPELLED   A. Ancient, interlacing script
___ 2. DECREED   B. Meditative; pondering
___ 3. HALTINGLY   C. Claws
___ 4. OMENS   D. Bursting with flame or smoke
___ 5. WRITHING   E. Dispersal
___ 6. BILLOWING   F. Without help
___ 7. UNAIDED   G. With hesitation
___ 8. HOARDS   H. Pagan; non-Christian
___ 9. HEATHEN   I. Trees with heart-shaped leaves
___ 10. HILT   J. Retaliation; revenge
___ 11. REPRISAL   K. Attributed; assigned
___ 12. SOLACE   L. Twisting and squirming
___ 13. BELCHING   M. Burning
___ 14. RUNIC   N. Rejoicing triumphantly
___ 15. ASCRIBED   O. Handle of a sword or dagger
___ 16. EXULTING   P. Discoloration of metal
___ 17. RUMINATIVE   Q. Make clear
___ 18. COBBLED   R. Stones roughly placed together
___ 19. ELUCIDATE   S. Signs of things to come
___ 20. TARNISH   T. Ordered by a judge
___ 21. CHARRING   U. Evil intent
___ 22. LINDEN   V. Comfort in sorrow
___ 23. DISSOLUTION   W. Flowing; rising on the winds
___ 24. TALONS   X. A group or accumulation
___ 25. MALICE   Y. Forced

Beowulf Vocabulary Matching 1 Answer Key

Y - 1. COMPELLED	A.	Ancient, interlacing script
T - 2. DECREED	B.	Meditative; pondering
G - 3. HALTINGLY	C.	Claws
S - 4. OMENS	D.	Bursting with flame or smoke
L - 5. WRITHING	E.	Dispersal
W - 6. BILLOWING	F.	Without help
F - 7. UNAIDED	G.	With hesitation
X - 8. HOARDS	H.	Pagan; non-Christian
H - 9. HEATHEN	I.	Trees with heart-shaped leaves
O -10. HILT	J.	Retaliation; revenge
J - 11. REPRISAL	K.	Attributed; assigned
V -12. SOLACE	L.	Twisting and squirming
D -13. BELCHING	M.	Burning
A -14. RUNIC	N.	Rejoicing triumphantly
K -15. ASCRIBED	O.	Handle of a sword or dagger
N -16. EXULTING	P.	Discoloration of metal
B -17. RUMINATIVE	Q.	Make clear
R -18. COBBLED	R.	Stones roughly placed together
Q -19. ELUCIDATE	S.	Signs of things to come
P -20. TARNISH	T.	Ordered by a judge
M -21. CHARRING	U.	Evil intent
I - 22. LINDEN	V.	Comfort in sorrow
E -23. DISSOLUTION	W.	Flowing; rising on the winds
C -24. TALONS	X.	A group or accumulation
U -25. MALICE	Y.	Forced

Beowulf Vocabulary Matching 2

___ 1. NIGGARDLY   A. Comfort in sorrow
___ 2. COBBLED   B. Searched for blindly
___ 3. ASCRIBED   C. Rejoicing triumphantly
___ 4. RUNIC   D. Anxiety or concern
___ 5. SOLICITUDE   E. Retaliation; revenge
___ 6. RUMINATIVE   F. Handle of a sword or dagger
___ 7. SCABBARD   G. Evil intent
___ 8. LINDEN   H. Attributed; assigned
___ 9. TAUT   I. Discoloration of metal
___10. BELCHING   J. Ordered by a judge
___11. BILLOWING   K. Trees with heart-shaped leaves
___12. DECREED   L. A group or accumulation
___13. TARNISH   M. Meditative; pondering
___14. HOARDS   N. Bursting with flame or smoke
___15. EXULTING   O. Dispersal
___16. HEATHEN   P. Sheath or cover for a sword
___17. GROPED   Q. Stingy
___18. MALICE   R. Tight
___19. REPRISAL   S. With hesitation
___20. SOLACE   T. Pagan; non-Christian
___21. HALTINGLY   U. Stones roughly placed together
___22. HILT   V. Ancient, interlacing script
___23. HAG   W. Flowing; rising on the winds
___24. DISSOLUTION   X. Pile of wood for burning dead bodies
___25. PYRE   Y. Repulsive old woman

Beowulf Vocabulary Matching 2 Answer Key

Q - 1. NIGGARDLY	A.	Comfort in sorrow
U - 2. COBBLED	B.	Searched for blindly
H - 3. ASCRIBED	C.	Rejoicing triumphantly
V - 4. RUNIC	D.	Anxiety or concern
D - 5. SOLICITUDE	E.	Retaliation; revenge
M - 6. RUMINATIVE	F.	Handle of a sword or dagger
P - 7. SCABBARD	G.	Evil intent
K - 8. LINDEN	H.	Attributed; assigned
R - 9. TAUT	I.	Discoloration of metal
N - 10. BELCHING	J.	Ordered by a judge
W - 11. BILLOWING	K.	Trees with heart-shaped leaves
J - 12. DECREED	L.	A group or accumulation
I - 13. TARNISH	M.	Meditative; pondering
L - 14. HOARDS	N.	Bursting with flame or smoke
C - 15. EXULTING	O.	Dispersal
T - 16. HEATHEN	P.	Sheath or cover for a sword
B - 17. GROPED	Q.	Stingy
G - 18. MALICE	R.	Tight
E - 19. REPRISAL	S.	With hesitation
A - 20. SOLACE	T.	Pagan; non-Christian
S - 21. HALTINGLY	U.	Stones roughly placed together
F - 22. HILT	V.	Ancient, interlacing script
Y - 23. HAG	W.	Flowing; rising on the winds
O - 24. DISSOLUTION	X.	Pile of wood for burning dead bodies
X - 25. PYRE	Y.	Repulsive old woman

Beowulf Vocabulary Matching 3

___ 1. WRETCHED   A. Handle of a sword or dagger
___ 2. CHARRING   B. Made of dirt
___ 3. DECREED   C. Without help
___ 4. HALTINGLY   D. With hesitation
___ 5. HILT   E. Trees with heart-shaped leaves
___ 6. HEATHEN   F. Twisting and squirming
___ 7. EARTHEN   G. Searched for blindly
___ 8. GROPED   H. Process of making amends
___ 9. EXULTING   I. Rejoicing triumphantly
___ 10. MALICE   J. Burning
___ 11. TAUT   K. Miserable; pitiable
___ 12. ASCRIBED   L. Bursting with flame or smoke
___ 13. BILLOWING   M. Narrow, trench-like depressions
___ 14. BELCHING   N. Pagan; non-Christian
___ 15. DISSOLUTION   O. Attributed; assigned
___ 16. FURROWS   P. Evil intent
___ 17. RUMINATIVE   Q. Stingy
___ 18. HOARDS   R. Claws
___ 19. TALONS   S. Tight
___ 20. WRITHING   T. Meditative; pondering
___ 21. LINDEN   U. Ordered by a judge
___ 22. REPARATION   V. Retaliation; revenge
___ 23. UNAIDED   W. A group or accumulation
___ 24. REPRISAL   X. Flowing; rising on the winds
___ 25. NIGGARDLY   Y. Dispersal

Beowulf Vocabulary Matching 3 Answer Key

K - 1.	WRETCHED	A.	Handle of a sword or dagger
J - 2.	CHARRING	B.	Made of dirt
U - 3.	DECREED	C.	Without help
D - 4.	HALTINGLY	D.	With hesitation
A - 5.	HILT	E.	Trees with heart-shaped leaves
N - 6.	HEATHEN	F.	Twisting and squirming
B - 7.	EARTHEN	G.	Searched for blindly
G - 8.	GROPED	H.	Process of making amends
I - 9.	EXULTING	I.	Rejoicing triumphantly
P - 10.	MALICE	J.	Burning
S - 11.	TAUT	K.	Miserable; pitiable
O - 12.	ASCRIBED	L.	Bursting with flame or smoke
X - 13.	BILLOWING	M.	Narrow, trench-like depressions
L - 14.	BELCHING	N.	Pagan; non-Christian
Y - 15.	DISSOLUTION	O.	Attributed; assigned
M - 16.	FURROWS	P.	Evil intent
T - 17.	RUMINATIVE	Q.	Stingy
W - 18.	HOARDS	R.	Claws
R - 19.	TALONS	S.	Tight
F - 20.	WRITHING	T.	Meditative; pondering
E - 21.	LINDEN	U.	Ordered by a judge
H - 22.	REPARATION	V.	Retaliation; revenge
C - 23.	UNAIDED	W.	A group or accumulation
V - 24.	REPRISAL	X.	Flowing; rising on the winds
Q - 25.	NIGGARDLY	Y.	Dispersal

Beowulf Vocabulary Matching 4

___ 1. RUMINATIVE   A. Ancient, interlacing script
___ 2. TRIPARTITE   B. Dispersal
___ 3. NIGGARDLY   C. Narrow, trench-like depressions
___ 4. TARNISH   D. Stingy
___ 5. HOARDS   E. Evil intent
___ 6. COMPELLED   F. Pagan; non-Christian
___ 7. JACKAL   G. Meditative; pondering
___ 8. EARTHEN   H. Poison
___ 9. REPRISAL   I. Sheath or cover for a sword
___10. CHARRING   J. Burning
___11. DISSOLUTION   K. Comfort in sorrow
___12. LINDEN   L. Tight
___13. HEATHEN   M. Consisting of three parts
___14. SOLICITUDE   N. Forced
___15. MALICE   O. Without help
___16. UNAIDED   P. Made of dirt
___17. TAUT   Q. Miserable; pitiable
___18. FURROWS   R. Discoloration of metal
___19. COBBLED   S. Anxiety or concern
___20. SCABBARD   T. Retaliation; revenge
___21. RUNIC   U. Stones roughly placed together
___22. OMENS   V. A group or accumulation
___23. VENOM   W. One who meanly serves the purpose of another
___24. SOLACE   X. Signs of things to come
___25. WRETCHED   Y. Trees with heart-shaped leaves

Beowulf Vocabulary Matching 4 Answer Key

G - 1. RUMINATIVE	A.	Ancient, interlacing script
M - 2. TRIPARTITE	B.	Dispersal
D - 3. NIGGARDLY	C.	Narrow, trench-like depressions
R - 4. TARNISH	D.	Stingy
V - 5. HOARDS	E.	Evil intent
N - 6. COMPELLED	F.	Pagan; non-Christian
W - 7. JACKAL	G.	Meditative; pondering
P - 8. EARTHEN	H.	Poison
T - 9. REPRISAL	I.	Sheath or cover for a sword
J - 10. CHARRING	J.	Burning
B - 11. DISSOLUTION	K.	Comfort in sorrow
Y - 12. LINDEN	L.	Tight
F - 13. HEATHEN	M.	Consisting of three parts
S - 14. SOLICITUDE	N.	Forced
E - 15. MALICE	O.	Without help
O - 16. UNAIDED	P.	Made of dirt
L - 17. TAUT	Q.	Miserable; pitiable
C - 18. FURROWS	R.	Discoloration of metal
U - 19. COBBLED	S.	Anxiety or concern
I - 20. SCABBARD	T.	Retaliation; revenge
A - 21. RUNIC	U.	Stones roughly placed together
X - 22. OMENS	V.	A group or accumulation
H - 23. VENOM	W.	One who meanly serves the purpose of another
K - 24. SOLACE	X.	Signs of things to come
Q - 25. WRETCHED	Y.	Trees with heart-shaped leaves

Beowulf Vocabulary Magic Squares 1

Match the definition with the vocabulary word. Put your answers in the magic squares below. When your answers are correct, all columns and rows will add to the same number.

A. MALICE
B. RUNIC
C. COMPELLED
D. CHARRING
E. REPRISAL
F. TALONS
G. RUMINATIVE
H. WRITHING
I. BILLOWING
J. SOLICITUDE
K. HALTINGLY
L. HILT
M. HEATHEN
N. COBBLED
O. GROPED
P. HAG

1. Evil intent
2. Stones roughly placed together
3. Anxiety or concern
4. Retaliation; revenge
5. Meditative; pondering
6. Handle of a sword or dagger
7. Repulsive old woman
8. Forced
9. Searched for blindly
10. Burning
11. Twisting and squirming
12. With hesitation
13. Flowing; rising on the winds
14. Claws
15. Ancient, interlacing script
16. Pagan; non-Christian

A=	B=	C=	D=
E=	F=	G=	H=
I=	J=	K=	L=
M=	N=	O=	P=

Beowulf Vocabulary Magic Squares 1 Answer Key

Match the definition with the vocabulary word. Put your answers in the magic squares below. When your answers are correct, all columns and rows will add to the same number.

A. MALICE
B. RUNIC
C. COMPELLED
D. CHARRING
E. REPRISAL
F. TALONS
G. RUMINATIVE
H. WRITHING
I. BILLOWING
J. SOLICITUDE
K. HALTINGLY
L. HILT
M. HEATHEN
N. COBBLED
O. GROPED
P. HAG

1. Evil intent
2. Stones roughly placed together
3. Anxiety or concern
4. Retaliation; revenge
5. Meditative; pondering
6. Handle of a sword or dagger
7. Repulsive old woman
8. Forced
9. Searched for blindly
10. Burning
11. Twisting and squirming
12. With hesitation
13. Flowing; rising on the winds
14. Claws
15. Ancient, interlacing script
16. Pagan; non-Christian

A=1	B=15	C=8	D=10
E=4	F=14	G=5	H=11
I=13	J=3	K=12	L=6
M=16	N=2	O=9	P=7

Beowulf Vocabulary Magic Squares 2

Match the definition with the vocabulary word. Put your answers in the magic squares below. When your answers are correct, all columns and rows will add to the same number.

A. MALICE
B. EMULATED
C. DECREED
D. DISSOLUTION
E. HILT
F. LINDEN
G. UNAIDED
H. EXULTING
I. TAUT
J. COMPELLED
K. RUNIC
L. ASCRIBED
M. HOARDS
N. TALONS
O. RUMINATIVE
P. ELUCIDATE

1. Claws
2. Without help
3. Attributed; assigned
4. Evil intent
5. Ancient, interlacing script
6. Rival with some degree of success
7. A group or accumulation
8. Rejoicing triumphantly
9. Handle of a sword or dagger
10. Make clear
11. Ordered by a judge
12. Forced
13. Dispersal
14. Tight
15. Trees with heart-shaped leaves
16. Meditative; pondering

A=	B=	C=	D=
E=	F=	G=	H=
I=	J=	K=	L=
M=	N=	O=	P=

Beowulf Vocabulary Magic Squares 2 Answer Key

Match the definition with the vocabulary word. Put your answers in the magic squares below. When your answers are correct, all columns and rows will add to the same number.

A. MALICE
B. EMULATED
C. DECREED
D. DISSOLUTION
E. HILT
F. LINDEN
G. UNAIDED
H. EXULTING
I. TAUT
J. COMPELLED
K. RUNIC
L. ASCRIBED
M. HOARDS
N. TALONS
O. RUMINATIVE
P. ELUCIDATE

1. Claws
2. Without help
3. Attributed; assigned
4. Evil intent
5. Ancient, interlacing script
6. Rival with some degree of success
7. A group or accumulation
8. Rejoicing triumphantly
9. Handle of a sword or dagger
10. Make clear
11. Ordered by a judge
12. Forced
13. Dispersal
14. Tight
15. Trees with heart-shaped leaves
16. Meditative; pondering

A=4	B=6	C=11	D=13
E=9	F=15	G=2	H=8
I=14	J=12	K=5	L=3
M=7	N=1	O=16	P=10

Beowulf Vocabulary Magic Squares 3

Match the definition with the vocabulary word. Put your answers in the magic squares below. When your answers are correct, all columns and rows will add to the same number.

A. SCABBARD
B. ELUCIDATE
C. TRIPARTITE
D. HOARDS
E. COMPELLED
F. HEATHEN
G. HAG
H. RUMINATIVE
I. TARNISH
J. WRETCHED
K. COBBLED
L. UNAIDED
M. BELCHING
N. RUNIC
O. JACKAL
P. HILT

1. One who meanly serves the purpose of another
2. A group or accumulation
3. Miserable; pitiable
4. Forced
5. Discoloration of metal
6. Pagan; non-Christian
7. Handle of a sword or dagger
8. Consisting of three parts
9. Meditative; pondering
10. Stones roughly placed together
11. Sheath or cover for a sword
12. Ancient, interlacing script
13. Make clear
14. Bursting with flame or smoke
15. Repulsive old woman
16. Without help

A=	B=	C=	D=
E=	F=	G=	H=
I=	J=	K=	L=
M=	N=	O=	P=

Beowulf Vocabulary Magic Squares 3 Answer Key

Match the definition with the vocabulary word. Put your answers in the magic squares below. When your answers are correct, all columns and rows will add to the same number.

A. SCABBARD
B. ELUCIDATE
C. TRIPARTITE
D. HOARDS
E. COMPELLED
F. HEATHEN
G. HAG
H. RUMINATIVE
I. TARNISH
J. WRETCHED
K. COBBLED
L. UNAIDED
M. BELCHING
N. RUNIC
O. JACKAL
P. HILT

1. One who meanly serves the purpose of another
2. A group or accumulation
3. Miserable; pitiable
4. Forced
5. Discoloration of metal
6. Pagan; non-Christian
7. Handle of a sword or dagger
8. Consisting of three parts
9. Meditative; pondering
10. Stones roughly placed together
11. Sheath or cover for a sword
12. Ancient, interlacing script
13. Make clear
14. Bursting with flame or smoke
15. Repulsive old woman
16. Without help

A=11	B=13	C=8	D=2
E=4	F=6	G=15	H=9
I=5	J=3	K=10	L=16
M=14	N=12	O=1	P=7

Beowulf Vocabulary Magic Squares 4

Match the definition with the vocabulary word. Put your answers in the magic squares below. When your answers are correct, all columns and rows will add to the same number.

A. PYRE
B. EMULATED
C. RUNIC
D. REPARATION
E. ASCRIBED
F. HOARDS
G. WRETCHED
H. LINDEN
I. GROPED
J. TALONS
K. VENOM
L. DISSOLUTION
M. FURROWS
N. SOLICITUDE
O. TRIPARTITE
P. SCABBARD

1. A group or accumulation
2. Searched for blindly
3. Consisting of three parts
4. Process of making amends
5. Narrow, trench-like depressions
6. Rival with some degree of success
7. Trees with heart-shaped leaves
8. Poison
9. Ancient, interlacing script
10. Sheath or cover for a sword
11. Claws
12. Attributed; assigned
13. Dispersal
14. Miserable; pitiable
15. Pile of wood for burning dead bodies
16. Anxiety or concern

A=	B=	C=	D=
E=	F=	G=	H=
I=	J=	K=	L=
M=	N=	O=	P=

Beowulf Vocabulary Magic Squares 4 Answer Key

Match the definition with the vocabulary word. Put your answers in the magic squares below. When your answers are correct, all columns and rows will add to the same number.

A. PYRE
B. EMULATED
C. RUNIC
D. REPARATION
E. ASCRIBED
F. HOARDS
G. WRETCHED
H. LINDEN
I. GROPED
J. TALONS
K. VENOM
L. DISSOLUTION
M. FURROWS
N. SOLICITUDE
O. TRIPARTITE
P. SCABBARD

1. A group or accumulation
2. Searched for blindly
3. Consisting of three parts
4. Process of making amends
5. Narrow, trench-like depressions
6. Rival with some degree of success
7. Trees with heart-shaped leaves
8. Poison
9. Ancient, interlacing script
10. Sheath or cover for a sword
11. Claws
12. Attributed; assigned
13. Dispersal
14. Miserable; pitiable
15. Pile of wood for burning dead bodies
16. Anxiety or concern

A=15	B=6	C=9	D=4
E=12	F=1	G=14	H=7
I=2	J=11	K=8	L=13
M=5	N=16	O=3	P=10

Beowulf Vocabulary Word Search 1

```
G E L U C I D A T E M A N U K V V Y Q P
R M K B N R B M R C B A S M N Y E F X P
O D T I I H Y Y I O S S L C S A P N F H
P T N L G R D Z P M R S K I R J I D O G
E B O L G X B N A P K U Q Y C I R D N M
D J I O A W N O R E Z B M F P E B I E L
Z W T W R S P I T L F P B I H K R E G D
S R A I D H Q T I L Q J V C N R J W D Q
B C R N L R J U T E Z X P F A A Z G G B
H T A G Y S K L E D N V C H E Y T N W K
W B P B J B W O R T E N C K M K X I R Y
H V E T B T Q S P Y D X Q Y U G J H V M
X W R A Q A T S S H V N Y U Z L P V C M E
T K D U T Q R I L A I N P L A C M L N B
W R E T C H E D S O L I C I T U D E R M
J P L Q S V E Y J Z A S T L J E I H B K Q
M I W N Y E F W I K S V O K I P D T N R F R
H S N G R F W I V T L G H N A O Y G N R
L A K C A J R V W R A R C E G C M S F T
N F E Y K P I Q F H C R H O S L D E F J
R D G Z E Q T Z Z B E P N N B R Y N N Q
K U P R N E H T R A E W O I A B S Y T S
W X N Y V M I J X B D L G O S W L X L Z
G K R I R T N H V J A T H Y R H F E P L
X T Z Q C E G Y P T F U R R O W S F D N
```

A group or accumulation (6)
Ancient, interlacing script (5)
Anxiety or concern (10)
Attributed; assigned (8)
Burning (8)
Bursting with flame or smoke (8)
Claws (6)
Comfort in sorrow (6)
Consisting of three parts (10)
Discoloration of metal (7)
Dispersal (11)
Evil intent (6)
Flowing; rising on the winds (9)
Forced (9)
Handle of a sword or dagger (4)
Made of dirt (7)
Make clear (9)
Meditative; pondering (10)
Miserable; pitiable (8)
Narrow, trench-like depressions (7)
One who meanly serves the purpose of another (6)
Ordered by a judge (7)

Pagan; non-Christian (7)
Pile of wood for burning dead bodies (4)
Poison (5)
Process of making amends (10)
Rejoicing triumphantly (8)
Repulsive old woman (3)
Retaliation; revenge (8)
Rival with some degree of success (8)
Searched for blindly (6)
Sheath or cover for a sword (8)
Signs of things to come (5)
Stingy (9)
Stones roughly placed together (7)
Tight (4)
Trees with heart-shaped leaves (6)
Twisting and squirming (8)
With hesitation (9)
Without help (7)

Beowulf Vocabulary Word Search 1 Answer Key

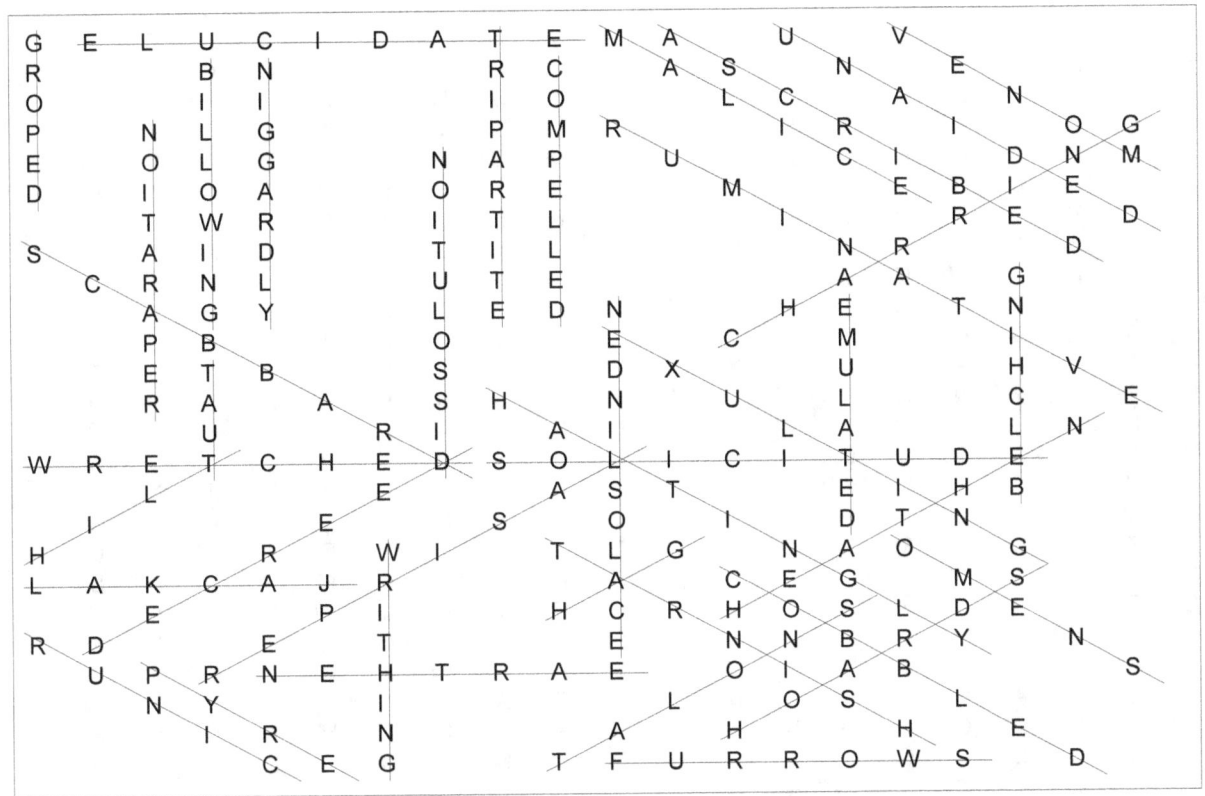

A group or accumulation (6)
Ancient, interlacing script (5)
Anxiety or concern (10)
Attributed; assigned (8)
Burning (8)
Bursting with flame or smoke (8)
Claws (6)
Comfort in sorrow (6)
Consisting of three parts (10)
Discoloration of metal (7)
Dispersal (11)
Evil intent (6)
Flowing; rising on the winds (9)
Forced (9)
Handle of a sword or dagger (4)
Made of dirt (7)
Make clear (9)
Meditative; pondering (10)
Miserable; pitiable (8)
Narrow, trench-like depressions (7)
One who meanly serves the purpose of another (6)
Ordered by a judge (7)

Pagan; non-Christian (7)
Pile of wood for burning dead bodies (4)
Poison (5)
Process of making amends (10)
Rejoicing triumphantly (8)
Repulsive old woman (3)
Retaliation; revenge (8)
Rival with some degree of success (8)
Searched for blindly (6)
Sheath or cover for a sword (8)
Signs of things to come (5)
Stingy (9)
Stones roughly placed together (7)
Tight (4)
Trees with heart-shaped leaves (6)
Twisting and squirming (8)
With hesitation (9)
Without help (7)

Beowulf Vocabulary Word Search 2

```
D E B I R C S A F Y Z V G N I H T I R W
E I J F F V L B S C S E B W Z A D G E Y
D H S V Z U H L E M K N M H Q L M F P R
I C O S K F R K D L H O B W B T S J A J
A E W A O F W R X E C M C G F I T A R C
N L F D R L E Z O G C H S B F N T C A H
U U V H M D U A Y W F R I W T G M K T J
N C C N A H S T R H S L E N L L D A I Y
T I R H T G G I T L U X E G Y N L O X
D D G U A R T G T O H Z Q T D E Z E N F
K A A G O R C H W V E S I H W R K G G
C T R P A I R I X L V D N T L Y P T N F
K E E Y N R N I L J E X A R P H P L R B
F D P U F G D W N L C E X A K H T K Q C
H Y R S G V D L L G H P S P Y P L B H N
K H I Q R F Q E Y N E D N I L J N J X S
G M S M S L P X P T V K H R N S H D H X
R Z A G X M T C D C D S Q T X F E W M C
N G L Z O K L R G C Z N P D D M S R A L
D E X C D W A F G O K O Y C U W F E L V
H C H Q P B Y J Z B P L P L R T G T I K
H A X T B G Y S M X A A W J L J C C D
T L R A R D G D M L L T A R N I S H E W
L O C Q C G D K B E E X F S M H N E W X
R S O L I C I T U D E O M E N S D D D B
```

A group or accumulation (6)
Ancient, interlacing script (5)
Anxiety or concern (10)
Attributed; assigned (8)
Burning (8)
Bursting with flame or smoke (8)
Claws (6)
Comfort in sorrow (6)
Consisting of three parts (10)
Discoloration of metal (7)
Dispersal (11)
Evil intent (6)
Flowing; rising on the winds (9)
Forced (9)
Handle of a sword or dagger (4)
Made of dirt (7)
Make clear (9)
Miserable; pitiable (8)
Narrow, trench-like depressions (7)
One who meanly serves the purpose of another (6)
Ordered by a judge (7)
Pagan; non-Christian (7)

Pile of wood for burning dead bodies (4)
Poison (5)
Process of making amends (10)
Rejoicing triumphantly (8)
Repulsive old woman (3)
Retaliation; revenge (8)
Rival with some degree of success (8)
Searched for blindly (6)
Sheath or cover for a sword (8)
Signs of things to come (5)
Stingy (9)
Stones roughly placed together (7)
Tight (4)
Trees with heart-shaped leaves (6)
Twisting and squirming (8)
With hesitation (9)
Without help (7)

Beowulf Vocabulary Word Search 2 Answer Key

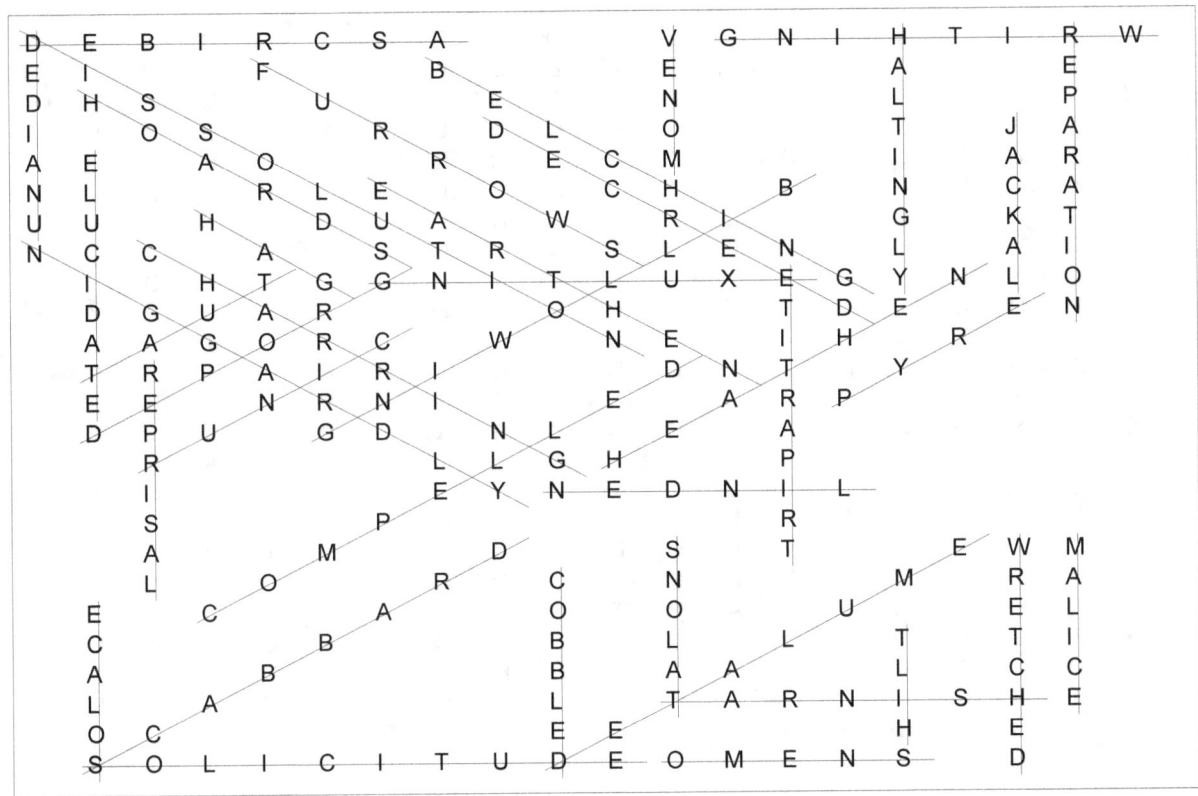

A group or accumulation (6)
Ancient, interlacing script (5)
Anxiety or concern (10)
Attributed; assigned (8)
Burning (8)
Bursting with flame or smoke (8)
Claws (6)
Comfort in sorrow (6)
Consisting of three parts (10)
Discoloration of metal (7)
Dispersal (11)
Evil intent (6)
Flowing; rising on the winds (9)
Forced (9)
Handle of a sword or dagger (4)
Made of dirt (7)
Make clear (9)
Miserable; pitiable (8)
Narrow, trench-like depressions (7)
One who meanly serves the purpose of another (6)
Ordered by a judge (7)
Pagan; non-Christian (7)

Pile of wood for burning dead bodies (4)
Poison (5)
Process of making amends (10)
Rejoicing triumphantly (8)
Repulsive old woman (3)
Retaliation; revenge (8)
Rival with some degree of success (8)
Searched for blindly (6)
Sheath or cover for a sword (8)
Signs of things to come (5)
Stingy (9)
Stones roughly placed together (7)
Tight (4)
Trees with heart-shaped leaves (6)
Twisting and squirming (8)
With hesitation (9)
Without help (7)

Beowulf Vocabulary Word Search 3

ASCRIBED
BELCHING
BILLOWING
CHARRING
COBBLED
COMPELLED
DECREED
DISSOLUTION
EARTHEN
ELUCIDATE

EMULATED
EXULTING
FURROWS
GROPED
HAG
HALTINGLY
HEATHEN
HILT
HOARDS
JACKAL

LINDEN
MALICE
NIGGARDLY
OMENS
PYRE
REPARATION
REPRISAL
RUMINATIVE
RUNIC
SCABBARD

SOLACE
SOLICITUDE
TALONS
TARNISH
TAUT
TRIPARTITE
UNAIDED
VENOM
WRETCHED
WRITHING

Beowulf Vocabulary Word Search 3 Answer Key

ASCRIBED	EMULATED	LINDEN	SOLACE
BELCHING	EXULTING	MALICE	SOLICITUDE
BILLOWING	FURROWS	NIGGARDLY	TALONS
CHARRING	GROPED	OMENS	TARNISH
COBBLED	HAG	PYRE	TAUT
COMPELLED	HALTINGLY	REPARATION	TRIPARTITE
DECREED	HEATHEN	REPRISAL	UNAIDED
DISSOLUTION	HILT	RUMINATIVE	VENOM
EARTHEN	HOARDS	RUNIC	WRETCHED
ELUCIDATE	JACKAL	SCABBARD	WRITHING

Beowulf Vocabulary Word Search 4

```
B N O I T U L O S S I D B E L C H I N G
P M M T G C S Q N J D R C D R P A Y R Z H
C C E C S B O O H E G I U U P A F E D M
C Q N H A G L B H C L J N T G R O P E D
R H S B A A Z C A P I I G N T L F R L C
E S A D T S T K M L C X C I W H L I L D
P C T R E C N N O E H D I O E N S E P J
A A A A R C H R I R D E L L O N D A P X
R B R W U I V I G S W L O J E N L M Z
A B N G L T N E G G J O S L P N R O R
T A I T G S D E E N E A D C L B Y W C L
I R S P N B N R U O D R L B Z F R F D
O D H H I E N E U T V M A D D J V Q E Y
N F L S H T K N M W R G O H L L F E H G
P K U S T M T F I U R I H B A Y T R V N
Y F A R I V F Q N Y L P P K C A Q Q W Q
Q E P F R S N Q A H L A C A D F H E K Q
H Z T H W O P D T H A A T I R G Y X Z K
R Z M N Q P W L I M J L C E H T C U H D
R R Q J Y S X S V J M U T L D P I L Y H
C X N X S J Y Y E X L Z J I C M V T H V
J P W M P S M W D E H S N Z N Y G I E X
C Z P K H G X G X H G M N F F G V N V Z
G N Y N T R W Z D Z H Q D R K T L G F P
F N G N M S Z G V B P G P D W M K Y N Y
```

ASCRIBED   EMULATED   LINDEN   SOLACE

BELCHING   EXULTING   MALICE   SOLICITUDE

BILLOWING   FURROWS   NIGGARDLY   TALONS

CHARRING   GROPED   OMENS   TARNISH

COBBLED   HAG   PYRE   TAUT

COMPELLED   HALTINGLY   REPARATION   TRIPARTITE

DECREED   HEATHEN   REPRISAL   UNAIDED

DISSOLUTION   HILT   RUMINATIVE   VENOM

EARTHEN   HOARDS   RUNIC   WRETCHED

ELUCIDATE   JACKAL   SCABBARD   WRITHING

Beowulf Vocabulary Word Search 4 Answer Key

ASCRIBED	EMULATED	LINDEN	SOLACE
BELCHING	EXULTING	MALICE	SOLICITUDE
BILLOWING	FURROWS	NIGGARDLY	TALONS
CHARRING	GROPED	OMENS	TARNISH
COBBLED	HAG	PYRE	TAUT
COMPELLED	HALTINGLY	REPARATION	TRIPARTITE
DECREED	HEATHEN	REPRISAL	UNAIDED
DISSOLUTION	HILT	RUMINATIVE	VENOM
EARTHEN	HOARDS	RUNIC	WRETCHED
ELUCIDATE	JACKAL	SCABBARD	WRITHING

Beowulf Vocabulary Crossword 1

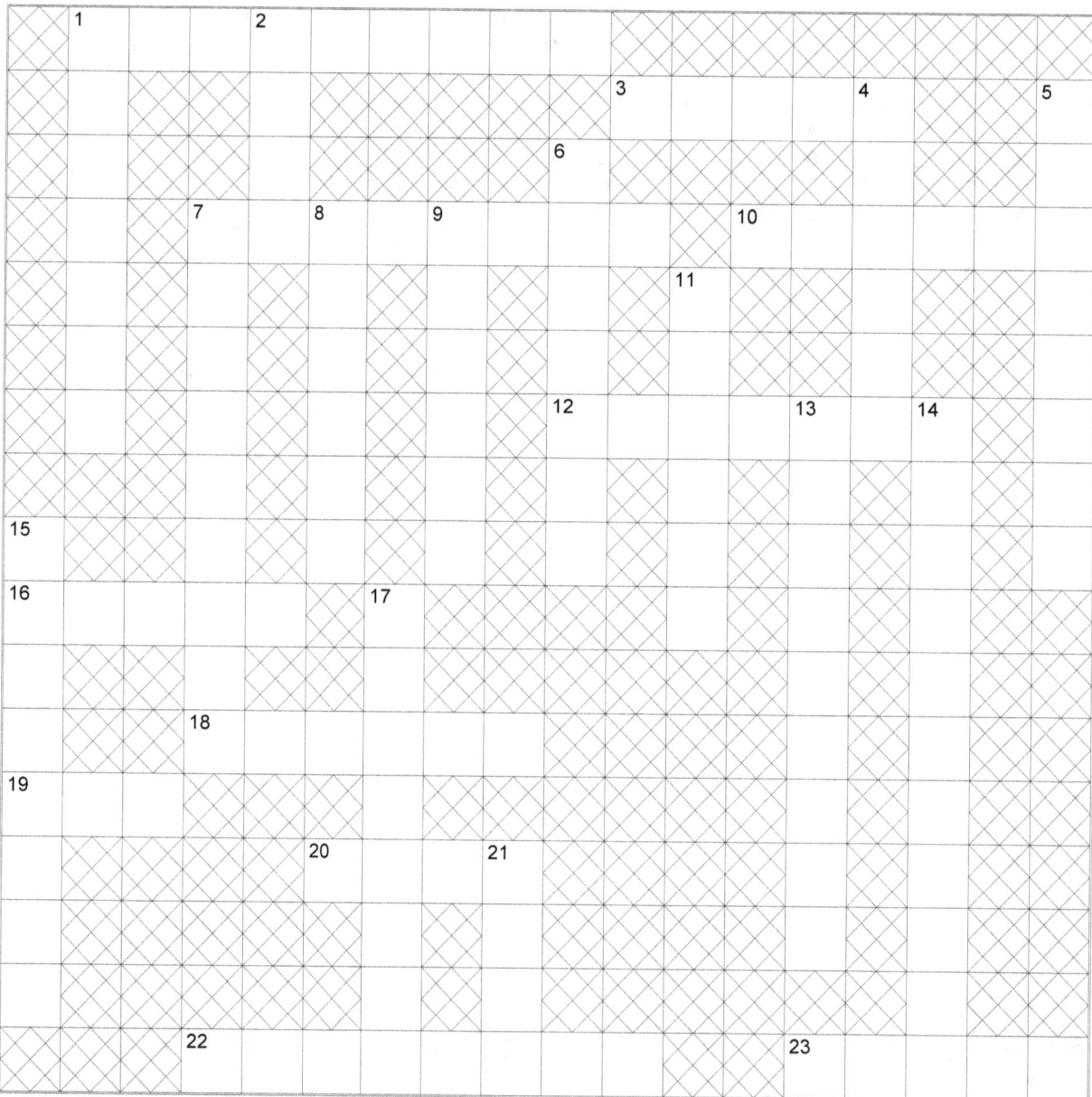

Across
1. Forced
3. Signs of things to come
7. Bursting with flame or smoke
10. Evil intent
12. Ordered by a judge
16. Ancient, interlacing script
18. Searched for blindly
19. Repulsive old woman
20. Handle of a sword or dagger
22. Rival with some degree of success
23. Poison

Down
1. Stones roughly placed together
2. Pile of wood for burning dead bodies
4. Comfort in sorrow
5. Miserable; pitiable
6. Without help
7. Flowing; rising on the winds
8. Trees with heart-shaped leaves
9. A group or accumulation
11. One who meanly serves the purpose of another
13. Make clear
14. Dispersal
15. Twisting and squirming
17. Retaliation; revenge
21. Tight

Beowulf Vocabulary Crossword 1 Answer Key

	1 C	O	M	2 P	E	L	L	E	D					
	O			Y				3 O	M	E	N	4 S		5 W
	B			R			6 U					O		R
	B	7 B	E	8 L	C	9 H	I	N	G	10 M	A	L	I	C	E
	L	I		I		O		A		11 J		A		T
	E	L		N		A		I		A		C		C
	D	L		D		R		12 D	E	C	R	13 E	14 D	H
		O		E		D		E		K		L		I	E
15 W		W		N		S		D		A		U		S	D
16 R	U	N	I	C		17 R				L		C		S	
I			N			E						I		O	
T		18 G	R	O	P	E	D					D		L	
19 H	A	G				R						A		U	
I				20 H	I	L	21 T					T		T	
N				S			A					E		I	
G				A			U							O	
		22 E	M	U	L	A	T	E	D			23 V	E	N	O	M

Across
1. Forced
3. Signs of things to come
7. Bursting with flame or smoke
10. Evil intent
12. Ordered by a judge
16. Ancient, interlacing script
18. Searched for blindly
19. Repulsive old woman
20. Handle of a sword or dagger
22. Rival with some degree of success
23. Poison

Down
1. Stones roughly placed together
2. Pile of wood for burning dead bodies
4. Comfort in sorrow
5. Miserable; pitiable
6. Without help
7. Flowing; rising on the winds
8. Trees with heart-shaped leaves
9. A group or accumulation
11. One who meanly serves the purpose of another
13. Make clear
14. Dispersal
15. Twisting and squirming
17. Retaliation; revenge
21. Tight

Beowulf Vocabulary Crossword 2

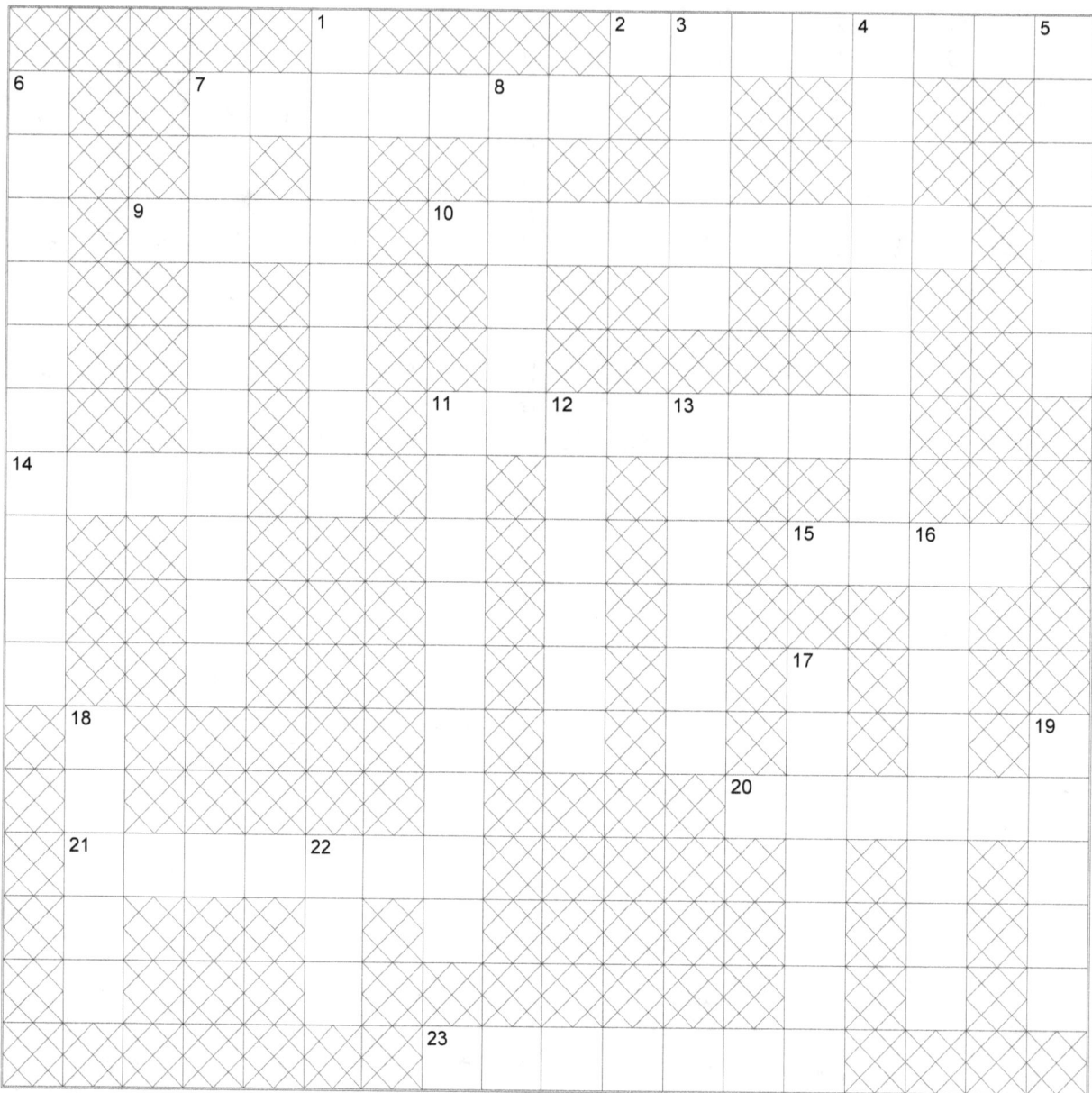

Across
2. Twisting and squirming
7. Discoloration of metal
9. Handle of a sword or dagger
10. Make clear
11. Bursting with flame or smoke
14. Tight
15. Pile of wood for burning dead bodies
20. Evil intent
21. Made of dirt
23. Ordered by a judge

Down
1. Miserable; pitiable
3. Ancient, interlacing script
4. With hesitation
5. Searched for blindly
6. Process of making amends
7. Consisting of three parts
8. Comfort in sorrow
11. Flowing; rising on the winds
12. Trees with heart-shaped leaves
13. A group or accumulation
16. Retaliation; revenge
17. Without help
18. Signs of things to come
19. Poison
22. Repulsive old woman

Beowulf Vocabulary Crossword 2 Answer Key

					1 W			2 W	3 R	I	4 T	H	I	5 G
6 R		7 T	A	R	N	I	8 S	H		U		A		R
E		R		E			O			N		L		O
P		9 H	I	L	T		10 E	L	U	C	I	D	A	T	E	P
A			P		C		A			C		I		E
R			A		H		C					N		D
A			R		E		11 B	12 E	L	13 C	H	I	N	G
14 T	A	U	T		D		I		I		O		L	
I			I				L		N		A		15 P	Y	16 R	E
O			T				L		D		R		E	
N			E				O		E		D		17 U		P
	18 O						W		N		S		N		19 V
	M						I					20 M	A	L	I	C	E
	21 E	A	R	T	22 H	E	N					I		S		N
	N				A		G					D		A		O
	S				G							E		L		M
					23 D	E	C	R	E	E	D			

Across
2. Twisting and squirming
7. Discoloration of metal
9. Handle of a sword or dagger
10. Make clear
11. Bursting with flame or smoke
14. Tight
15. Pile of wood for burning dead bodies
20. Evil intent
21. Made of dirt
23. Ordered by a judge

Down
1. Miserable; pitiable
3. Ancient, interlacing script
4. With hesitation
5. Searched for blindly
6. Process of making amends
7. Consisting of three parts
8. Comfort in sorrow
11. Flowing; rising on the winds
12. Trees with heart-shaped leaves
13. A group or accumulation
16. Retaliation; revenge
17. Without help
18. Signs of things to come
19. Poison
22. Repulsive old woman

Beowulf Vocabulary Crossword 3

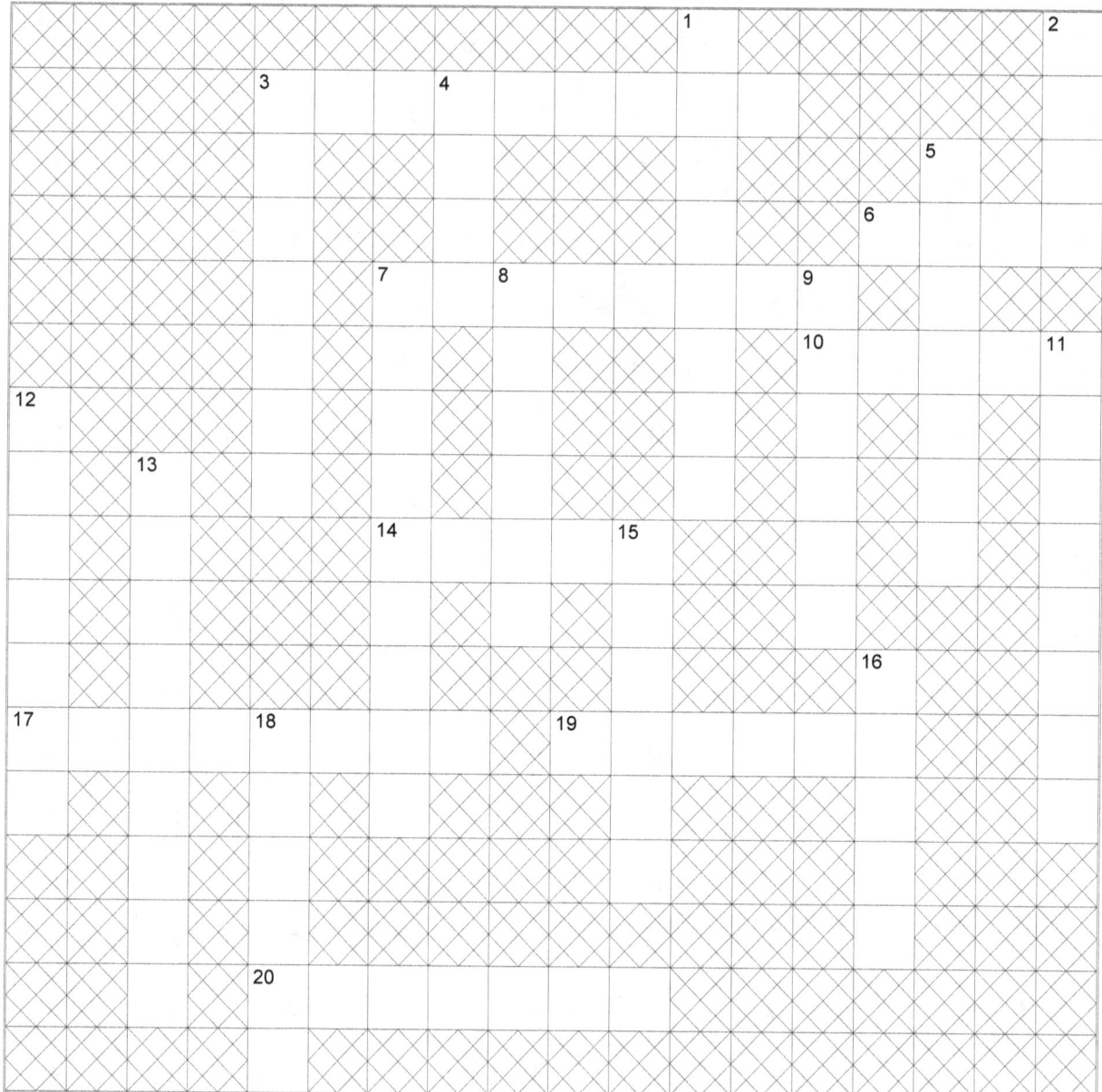

Across
3. Forced
6. Tight
7. Bursting with flame or smoke
10. Ancient, interlacing script
14. Signs of things to come
17. Twisting and squirming
19. Evil intent
20. Ordered by a judge

Down
1. Retaliation; revenge
2. Handle of a sword or dagger
3. Stones roughly placed together
4. Pile of wood for burning dead bodies
5. Discoloration of metal
7. Flowing; rising on the winds
8. Trees with heart-shaped leaves
9. Searched for blindly
11. Burning
12. Narrow, trench-like depressions
13. Make clear
15. Comfort in sorrow
16. Poison
18. A group or accumulation

Beowulf Vocabulary Crossword 3 Answer Key

								¹R				²H
		³C	O	M	⁴P	E	L	L	E	D		I
		O			Y			P			⁵T	L
		B			R			R		⁶T	A	U	T
		B		⁷B	⁸E	L	C	H	I	N	⁹G	
		L		I	L	I		S		¹⁰R	U	N	I	¹¹C
¹²F		E		L		N		A		O		I		H
U	¹³E	D		L		D		L		P		S		A
R	L		¹⁴O	M	E	N	¹⁵S			E		H		R
R	U		M			N	O			D				R
O	C		I				L			¹⁶V				I
¹⁷W	R	I	T	¹⁸H	I	N	G	¹⁹M	A	L	I	C	E	N
S	D		O	G				C				N		G
	A			A				E				O		
	T			R								M		
	E		²⁰D	E	C	R	E	E	D					
			S											

Across
3. Forced
6. Tight
7. Bursting with flame or smoke
10. Ancient, interlacing script
14. Signs of things to come
17. Twisting and squirming
19. Evil intent
20. Ordered by a judge

Down
1. Retaliation; revenge
2. Handle of a sword or dagger
3. Stones roughly placed together
4. Pile of wood for burning dead bodies
5. Discoloration of metal
7. Flowing; rising on the winds
8. Trees with heart-shaped leaves
9. Searched for blindly
11. Burning
12. Narrow, trench-like depressions
13. Make clear
15. Comfort in sorrow
16. Poison
18. A group or accumulation

Beowulf Vocabulary Crossword 4

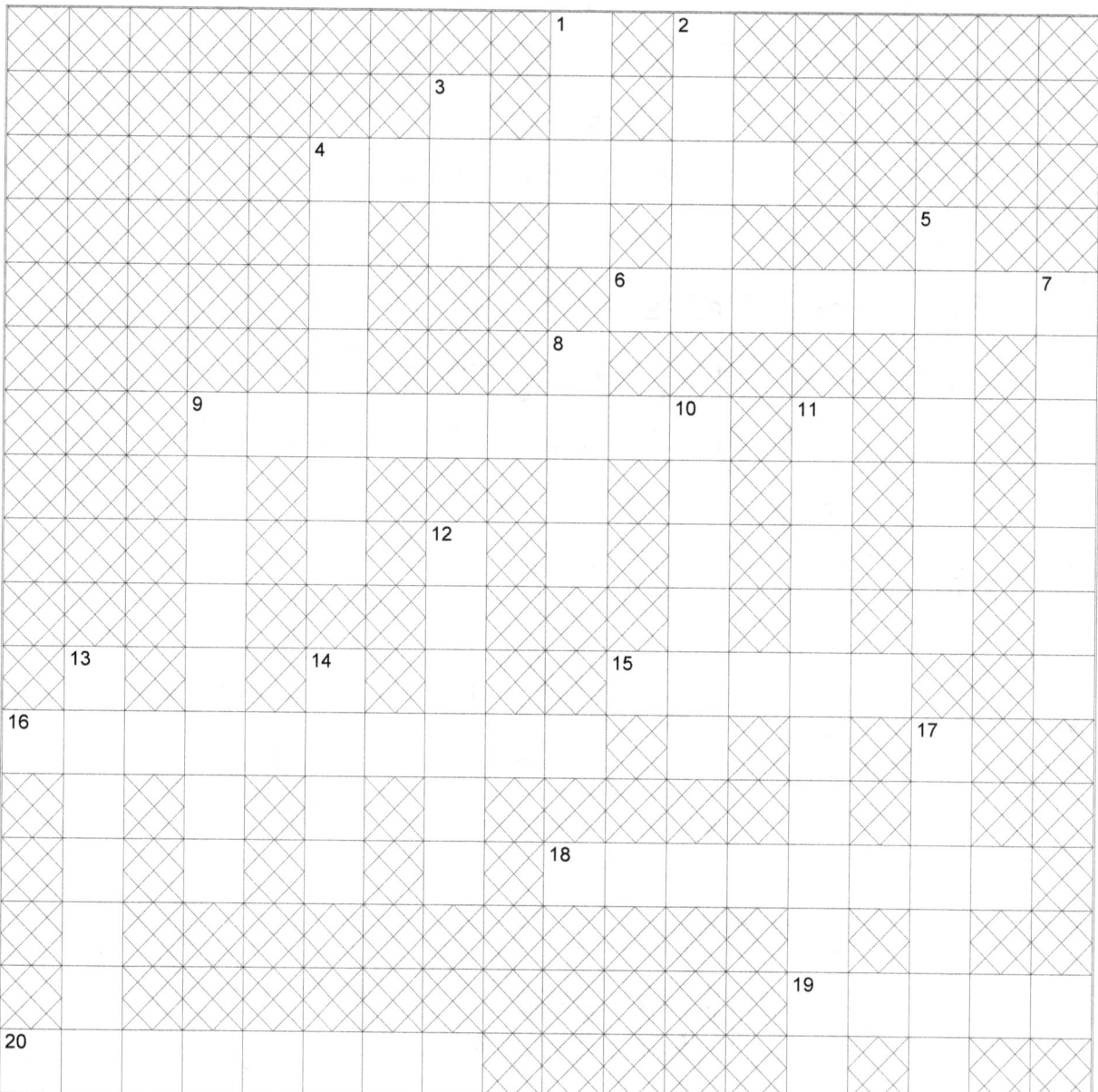

Across
4. Burning
6. Sheath or cover for a sword
9. Flowing; rising on the winds
15. Poison
16. Meditative; pondering
18. Rejoicing triumphantly
19. Signs of things to come
20. Attributed; assigned

Down
1. Pile of wood for burning dead bodies
2. Ancient, interlacing script
3. Repulsive old woman
4. Stones roughly placed together
5. Made of dirt
7. Ordered by a judge
8. Handle of a sword or dagger
9. Bursting with flame or smoke
10. Searched for blindly
11. Dispersal
12. Evil intent
13. Narrow, trench-like depressions
14. Tight
17. Trees with heart-shaped leaves

Beowulf Vocabulary Crossword 4 Answer Key

Across
4. Burning
6. Sheath or cover for a sword
9. Flowing; rising on the winds
15. Poison
16. Meditative; pondering
18. Rejoicing triumphantly
19. Signs of things to come
20. Attributed; assigned

Down
1. Pile of wood for burning dead bodies
2. Ancient, interlacing script
3. Repulsive old woman
4. Stones roughly placed together
5. Made of dirt
7. Ordered by a judge
8. Handle of a sword or dagger
9. Bursting with flame or smoke
10. Searched for blindly
11. Dispersal
12. Evil intent
13. Narrow, trench-like depressions
14. Tight
17. Trees with heart-shaped leaves

Beowulf Vocabulary Juggle Letters 1

1. DGREPO = 1. _____
Searched for blindly

2. NGRRCIAH = 2. _____
Burning

3. DABCRSAB = 3. _____
Sheath or cover for a sword

4. EBLHNGCI = 4. _____
Bursting with flame or smoke

5. CERDEED = 5. _____
Ordered by a judge

6. ETHHAEN = 6. _____
Pagan; non-Christian

7. YERP = 7. _____
Pile of wood for burning dead bodies

8. ADNEIDU = 8. _____
Without help

9. ILMAEC = 9. _____
Evil intent

10. IHTL =10. _____
Handle of a sword or dagger

11. PELDELMCO =11. _____
Forced

12. ILLHANGTY =12. _____
With hesitation

13. SIRPAERL =13. _____
Retaliation; revenge

14. OSHARD =14. _____
A group or accumulation

15. NTIHASR =15. _____
Discoloration of metal

Beowulf Vocabulary Juggle Letters 1 Answer Key

1. DGREPO = 1. GROPED
Searched for blindly

2. NGRRCIAH = 2. CHARRING
Burning

3. DABCRSAB = 3. SCABBARD
Sheath or cover for a sword

4. EBLHNGCI = 4. BELCHING
Bursting with flame or smoke

5. CERDEED = 5. DECREED
Ordered by a judge

6. ETHHAEN = 6. HEATHEN
Pagan; non-Christian

7. YERP = 7. PYRE
Pile of wood for burning dead bodies

8. ADNEIDU = 8. UNAIDED
Without help

9. ILMAEC = 9. MALICE
Evil intent

10. IHTL = 10. HILT
Handle of a sword or dagger

11. PELDELMCO = 11. COMPELLED
Forced

12. ILLHANGTY = 12. HALTINGLY
With hesitation

13. SIRPAERL = 13. REPRISAL
Retaliation; revenge

14. OSHARD = 14. HOARDS
A group or accumulation

15. NTIHASR = 15. TARNISH
Discoloration of metal

Beowulf Vocabulary Juggle Letters 2

1. CEDDREE = 1. _____
   Ordered by a judge

2. SLNOTA = 2. _____
   Claws

3. NCLIGEHB = 3. _____
   Bursting with flame or smoke

4. SLSTONUODII = 4. _____
   Dispersal

5. IDLAGYRNG = 5. _____
   Stingy

6. INTAUMERIV = 6. _____
   Meditative; pondering

7. IELNDN = 7. _____
   Trees with heart-shaped leaves

8. ALTNYILHG = 8. _____
   With hesitation

9. BLDBCOE = 9. _____
   Stones roughly placed together

10. SAEPLRIR = 10. _____
    Retaliation; revenge

11. NMOEV = 11. _____
    Poison

12. ANHTEEH = 12. _____
    Pagan; non-Christian

13. DLMTAUEE = 13. _____
    Rival with some degree of success

14. RIGCANRH = 14. _____
    Burning

15. CMLAIE = 15. _____
    Evil intent

Beowulf Vocabulary Juggle Letters 2 Answer Key

1. CEDDREE = 1. DECREED
Ordered by a judge

2. SLNOTA = 2. TALONS
Claws

3. NCLIGEHB = 3. BELCHING
Bursting with flame or smoke

4. SLSTONUODII = 4. DISSOLUTION
Dispersal

5. IDLAGYRNG = 5. NIGGARDLY
Stingy

6. INTAUMERIV = 6. RUMINATIVE
Meditative; pondering

7. IELNDN = 7. LINDEN
Trees with heart-shaped leaves

8. ALTNYILHG = 8. HALTINGLY
With hesitation

9. BLDBCOE = 9. COBBLED
Stones roughly placed together

10. SAEPLRIR =10. REPRISAL
Retaliation; revenge

11. NMOEV =11. VENOM
Poison

12. ANHTEEH =12. HEATHEN
Pagan; non-Christian

13. DLMTAUEE =13. EMULATED
Rival with some degree of success

14. RIGCANRH =14. CHARRING
Burning

15. CMLAIE =15. MALICE
Evil intent

Copyrighted

Beowulf Vocabulary Juggle Letters 3

1. MESON = 1. _____
Signs of things to come

2. OEMNV = 2. _____
Poison

3. AIRNRHCG = 3. _____
Burning

4. UATT = 4. _____
Tight

5. UDEILECAT = 5. _____
Make clear

6. EEATRNH = 6. _____
Made of dirt

7. IGHYLALTN = 7. _____
With hesitation

8. ETHHNEA = 8. _____
Pagan; non-Christian

9. SONLAT = 9. _____
Claws

10. ILTH = 10. _____
Handle of a sword or dagger

11. DETHERCW = 11. _____
Miserable; pitiable

12. EYRP = 12. _____
Pile of wood for burning dead bodies

13. RTREAPTIIT = 13. _____
Consisting of three parts

14. DIENNL = 14. _____
Trees with heart-shaped leaves

15. DUDNEIA = 15. _____
Without help

Beowulf Vocabulary Juggle Letters 3 Answer Key

1. MESON = 1. OMENS
   Signs of things to come

2. OEMNV = 2. VENOM
   Poison

3. AIRNRHCG = 3. CHARRING
   Burning

4. UATT = 4. TAUT
   Tight

5. UDEILECAT = 5. ELUCIDATE
   Make clear

6. EEATRNH = 6. EARTHEN
   Made of dirt

7. IGHYLALTN = 7. HALTINGLY
   With hesitation

8. ETHHNEA = 8. HEATHEN
   Pagan; non-Christian

9. SONLAT = 9. TALONS
   Claws

10. ILTH =10. HILT
    Handle of a sword or dagger

11. DETHERCW =11. WRETCHED
    Miserable; pitiable

12. EYRP =12. PYRE
    Pile of wood for burning dead bodies

13. RTREAPTIIT =13. TRIPARTITE
    Consisting of three parts

14. DIENNL =14. LINDEN
    Trees with heart-shaped leaves

15. DUDNEIA =15. UNAIDED
    Without help

Beowulf Vocabulary Juggle Letters 4

1. IRTIWNHG = 1. _____
   Twisting and squirming

2. APAORNRTEI = 2. _____
   Process of making amends

3. SLATON = 3. _____
   Claws

4. KAJLCA = 4. _____
   One who meanly serves the purpose of another

5. IGUXLNTE = 5. _____
   Rejoicing triumphantly

6. AHG = 6. _____
   Repulsive old woman

7. INLEND = 7. _____
   Trees with heart-shaped leaves

8. NGIRCRAH = 8. _____
   Burning

9. OILNSODTUSI = 9. _____
   Dispersal

10. TIPATRREIT = 10. _____
    Consisting of three parts

11. EODBCBL = 11. _____
    Stones roughly placed together

12. HLIT = 12. _____
    Handle of a sword or dagger

13. NCLIGBEH = 13. _____
    Bursting with flame or smoke

14. NDUEDAI = 14. _____
    Without help

15. RASDHO = 15. _____
    A group or accumulation

Beowulf Vocabulary Juggle Letters 4 Answer Key

1. IRTIWNHG = 1. WRITHING
Twisting and squirming

2. APAORNRTEI = 2. REPARATION
Process of making amends

3. SLATON = 3. TALONS
Claws

4. KAJLCA = 4. JACKAL
One who meanly serves the purpose of another

5. IGUXLNTE = 5. EXULTING
Rejoicing triumphantly

6. AHG = 6. HAG
Repulsive old woman

7. INLEND = 7. LINDEN
Trees with heart-shaped leaves

8. NGIRCRAH = 8. CHARRING
Burning

9. OILNSODTUSI = 9. DISSOLUTION
Dispersal

10. TIPATRREIT = 10. TRIPARTITE
Consisting of three parts

11. EODBCBL = 11. COBBLED
Stones roughly placed together

12. HLIT = 12. HILT
Handle of a sword or dagger

13. NCLIGBEH = 13. BELCHING
Bursting with flame or smoke

14. NDUEDAI = 14. UNAIDED
Without help

15. RASDHO = 15. HOARDS
A group or accumulation

ASCRIBED	Attributed; assigned
BELCHING	Bursting with flame or smoke
BILLOWING	Flowing; rising on the winds
CHARRING	Burning
COBBLED	Stones roughly placed together
COMPELLED	Forced

DECREED	Ordered by a judge
DISSOLUTION	Dispersal
EARTHEN	Made of dirt
ELUCIDATE	Make clear
EMULATED	Rival with some degree of success
EXULTING	Rejoicing triumphantly

FURROWS	Narrow, trench-like depressions
GROPED	Searched for blindly
HAG	Repulsive old woman
HALTINGLY	With hesitation
HEATHEN	Pagan; non-Christian
HILT	Handle of a sword or dagger

HOARDS	A group or accumulation
JACKAL	One who meanly serves the purpose of another
LINDEN	Trees with heart-shaped leaves
MALICE	Evil intent
NIGGARDLY	Stingy
OMENS	Signs of things to come

PYRE	Pile of wood for burning dead bodies
REPARATION	Process of making amends
REPRISAL	Retaliation; revenge
RUMINATIVE	Meditative; pondering
RUNIC	Ancient, interlacing script
SCABBARD	Sheath or cover for a sword

SOLACE	Comfort in sorrow
SOLICITUDE	Anxiety or concern
TALONS	Claws
TARNISH	Discoloration of metal
TAUT	Tight
TRIPARTITE	Consisting of three parts

UNAIDED	Without help
VENOM	Poison
WRETCHED	Miserable; pitiable
WRITHING	Twisting and squirming

Beowulf Vocabulary

LINDEN	RUMINATIVE	EXULTING	HILT	HEATHEN
FURROWS	HOARDS	EARTHEN	TAUT	NIGGARDLY
SOLICITUDE	WRETCHED	FREE SPACE	TRIPARTITE	BILLOWING
MALICE	OMENS	VENOM	GROPED	TALONS
REPARATION	RUNIC	PYRE	ELUCIDATE	HAG

Beowulf Vocabulary

EMULATED	BELCHING	TARNISH	COMPELLED	REPRISAL
WRITHING	DISSOLUTION	JACKAL	ASCRIBED	SOLACE
HALTINGLY	COBBLED	FREE SPACE	DECREED	UNAIDED
HAG	ELUCIDATE	PYRE	RUNIC	REPARATION
TALONS	GROPED	VENOM	OMENS	MALICE

Beowulf Vocabulary

HALTINGLY	WRITHING	TAUT	COMPELLED	COBBLED
EXULTING	LINDEN	SOLICITUDE	TRIPARTITE	TALONS
UNAIDED	ELUCIDATE	FREE SPACE	BELCHING	WRETCHED
HAG	PYRE	ASCRIBED	OMENS	HILT
GROPED	RUMINATIVE	DISSOLUTION	REPARATION	FURROWS

Beowulf Vocabulary

HEATHEN	SOLACE	REPRISAL	TARNISH	CHARRING
JACKAL	MALICE	SCABBARD	BILLOWING	RUNIC
VENOM	EMULATED	FREE SPACE	NIGGARDLY	HOARDS
FURROWS	REPARATION	DISSOLUTION	RUMINATIVE	GROPED
HILT	OMENS	ASCRIBED	PYRE	HAG

Beowulf Vocabulary

HILT	SOLACE	OMENS	HAG	HALTINGLY
TALONS	HEATHEN	WRETCHED	UNAIDED	GROPED
EMULATED	JACKAL	FREE SPACE	PYRE	REPARATION
BELCHING	EARTHEN	REPRISAL	DISSOLUTION	LINDEN
MALICE	TRIPARTITE	DECREED	CHARRING	SOLICITUDE

Beowulf Vocabulary

BILLOWING	COBBLED	ELUCIDATE	TAUT	VENOM
HOARDS	COMPELLED	WRITHING	RUNIC	SCABBARD
ASCRIBED	FURROWS	FREE SPACE	EXULTING	RUMINATIVE
SOLICITUDE	CHARRING	DECREED	TRIPARTITE	MALICE
LINDEN	DISSOLUTION	REPRISAL	EARTHEN	BELCHING

Beowulf Vocabulary

MALICE	JACKAL	GROPED	TAUT	RUNIC
NIGGARDLY	SOLACE	TALONS	REPRISAL	ASCRIBED
SCABBARD	REPARATION	FREE SPACE	HALTINGLY	HILT
LINDEN	UNAIDED	OMENS	HOARDS	WRITHING
PYRE	HEATHEN	TARNISH	RUMINATIVE	EMULATED

Beowulf Vocabulary

BILLOWING	CHARRING	EXULTING	COMPELLED	HAG
SOLICITUDE	BELCHING	TRIPARTITE	DISSOLUTION	EARTHEN
VENOM	ELUCIDATE	FREE SPACE	DECREED	COBBLED
EMULATED	RUMINATIVE	TARNISH	HEATHEN	PYRE
WRITHING	HOARDS	OMENS	UNAIDED	LINDEN

Beowulf Vocabulary

SOLICITUDE	TALONS	GROPED	HAG	JACKAL
ASCRIBED	TARNISH	HALTINGLY	ELUCIDATE	HOARDS
EARTHEN	DECREED	FREE SPACE	RUNIC	TAUT
COMPELLED	DISSOLUTION	NIGGARDLY	MALICE	VENOM
CHARRING	EXULTING	REPARATION	BILLOWING	HILT

Beowulf Vocabulary

PYRE	FURROWS	SCABBARD	RUMINATIVE	SOLACE
WRETCHED	LINDEN	OMENS	BELCHING	REPRISAL
WRITHING	EMULATED	FREE SPACE	TRIPARTITE	COBBLED
HILT	BILLOWING	REPARATION	EXULTING	CHARRING
VENOM	MALICE	NIGGARDLY	DISSOLUTION	COMPELLED

Beowulf Vocabulary

REPARATION	ASCRIBED	HILT	TRIPARTITE	ELUCIDATE
MALICE	SCABBARD	UNAIDED	LINDEN	HALTINGLY
HOARDS	EMULATED	FREE SPACE	VENOM	DECREED
TAUT	WRITHING	EXULTING	TALONS	BILLOWING
FURROWS	COMPELLED	DISSOLUTION	BELCHING	OMENS

Beowulf Vocabulary

REPRISAL	PYRE	WRETCHED	CHARRING	NIGGARDLY
SOLICITUDE	TARNISH	SOLACE	EARTHEN	JACKAL
COBBLED	HEATHEN	FREE SPACE	GROPED	HAG
OMENS	BELCHING	DISSOLUTION	COMPELLED	FURROWS
BILLOWING	TALONS	EXULTING	WRITHING	TAUT

Beowulf Vocabulary

RUNIC	REPRISAL	OMENS	DISSOLUTION	REPARATION
COMPELLED	HAG	MALICE	FURROWS	HALTINGLY
SCABBARD	ELUCIDATE	FREE SPACE	PYRE	TAUT
CHARRING	GROPED	TALONS	EXULTING	WRETCHED
DECREED	NIGGARDLY	COBBLED	HOARDS	SOLACE

Beowulf Vocabulary

EARTHEN	EMULATED	HILT	TARNISH	UNAIDED
ASCRIBED	VENOM	TRIPARTITE	BILLOWING	LINDEN
WRITHING	RUMINATIVE	FREE SPACE	JACKAL	HEATHEN
SOLACE	HOARDS	COBBLED	NIGGARDLY	DECREED
WRETCHED	EXULTING	TALONS	GROPED	CHARRING

Beowulf Vocabulary

EXULTING	TAUT	ELUCIDATE	BELCHING	COBBLED
ASCRIBED	HEATHEN	HAG	TARNISH	HOARDS
EMULATED	CHARRING	FREE SPACE	LINDEN	PYRE
EARTHEN	UNAIDED	BILLOWING	REPRISAL	SOLACE
SOLICITUDE	VENOM	RUNIC	REPARATION	WRITHING

Beowulf Vocabulary

HALTINGLY	FURROWS	WRETCHED	TALONS	MALICE
DISSOLUTION	DECREED	TRIPARTITE	NIGGARDLY	SCABBARD
OMENS	COMPELLED	FREE SPACE	GROPED	RUMINATIVE
WRITHING	REPARATION	RUNIC	VENOM	SOLICITUDE
SOLACE	REPRISAL	BILLOWING	UNAIDED	EARTHEN

Beowulf Vocabulary

EARTHEN	EXULTING	DECREED	RUMINATIVE	ELUCIDATE
MALICE	HALTINGLY	TRIPARTITE	TALONS	CHARRING
OMENS	PYRE	FREE SPACE	FURROWS	VENOM
JACKAL	SCABBARD	TARNISH	GROPED	BILLOWING
HILT	SOLICITUDE	HAG	ASCRIBED	COBBLED

Beowulf Vocabulary

BELCHING	COMPELLED	LINDEN	TAUT	REPRISAL
WRITHING	DISSOLUTION	SOLACE	NIGGARDLY	UNAIDED
REPARATION	HEATHEN	FREE SPACE	HOARDS	WRETCHED
COBBLED	ASCRIBED	HAG	SOLICITUDE	HILT
BILLOWING	GROPED	TARNISH	SCABBARD	JACKAL

Beowulf Vocabulary

OMENS	UNAIDED	SCABBARD	COBBLED	BELCHING
COMPELLED	HEATHEN	VENOM	JACKAL	HOARDS
LINDEN	HILT	FREE SPACE	TRIPARTITE	TALONS
FURROWS	TAUT	ASCRIBED	RUNIC	MALICE
RUMINATIVE	ELUCIDATE	SOLACE	EXULTING	HAG

Beowulf Vocabulary

EARTHEN	GROPED	EMULATED	WRITHING	DISSOLUTION
NIGGARDLY	REPRISAL	SOLICITUDE	REPARATION	TARNISH
DECREED	BILLOWING	FREE SPACE	HALTINGLY	CHARRING
HAG	EXULTING	SOLACE	ELUCIDATE	RUMINATIVE
MALICE	RUNIC	ASCRIBED	TAUT	FURROWS

Beowulf Vocabulary

HALTINGLY	ELUCIDATE	SOLICITUDE	VENOM	EXULTING
TARNISH	DECREED	RUNIC	RUMINATIVE	WRITHING
FURROWS	ASCRIBED	FREE SPACE	HEATHEN	WRETCHED
EMULATED	NIGGARDLY	CHARRING	LINDEN	COBBLED
REPRISAL	COMPELLED	BELCHING	SOLACE	DISSOLUTION

Beowulf Vocabulary

EARTHEN	PYRE	JACKAL	BILLOWING	HOARDS
GROPED	TAUT	HILT	SCABBARD	TALONS
OMENS	MALICE	FREE SPACE	REPARATION	UNAIDED
DISSOLUTION	SOLACE	BELCHING	COMPELLED	REPRISAL
COBBLED	LINDEN	CHARRING	NIGGARDLY	EMULATED

Beowulf Vocabulary

HAG	NIGGARDLY	EARTHEN	CHARRING	RUMINATIVE
SOLACE	ELUCIDATE	WRETCHED	BILLOWING	UNAIDED
TAUT	TRIPARTITE	FREE SPACE	COBBLED	OMENS
FURROWS	HEATHEN	GROPED	LINDEN	ASCRIBED
WRITHING	BELCHING	COMPELLED	REPRISAL	SOLICITUDE

Beowulf Vocabulary

EXULTING	HALTINGLY	HILT	MALICE	EMULATED
DISSOLUTION	HOARDS	JACKAL	TALONS	RUNIC
VENOM	REPARATION	FREE SPACE	DECREED	SCABBARD
SOLICITUDE	REPRISAL	COMPELLED	BELCHING	WRITHING
ASCRIBED	LINDEN	GROPED	HEATHEN	FURROWS

Beowulf Vocabulary

COMPELLED	MALICE	TAUT	EARTHEN	TALONS
SCABBARD	SOLACE	DISSOLUTION	HILT	COBBLED
OMENS	EXULTING	FREE SPACE	HEATHEN	NIGGARDLY
ELUCIDATE	HAG	RUNIC	EMULATED	GROPED
HALTINGLY	JACKAL	RUMINATIVE	LINDEN	TRIPARTITE

Beowulf Vocabulary

BELCHING	FURROWS	HOARDS	BILLOWING	WRETCHED
CHARRING	SOLICITUDE	REPRISAL	VENOM	DECREED
ASCRIBED	TARNISH	FREE SPACE	WRITHING	PYRE
TRIPARTITE	LINDEN	RUMINATIVE	JACKAL	HALTINGLY
GROPED	EMULATED	RUNIC	HAG	ELUCIDATE

Beowulf Vocabulary

EARTHEN	COBBLED	SOLACE	LINDEN	EXULTING
RUNIC	REPRISAL	FURROWS	ELUCIDATE	GROPED
TARNISH	OMENS	FREE SPACE	COMPELLED	NIGGARDLY
DECREED	RUMINATIVE	CHARRING	BILLOWING	DISSOLUTION
ASCRIBED	WRETCHED	HAG	HEATHEN	SOLICITUDE

Beowulf Vocabulary

BELCHING	TALONS	TAUT	UNAIDED	JACKAL
SCABBARD	EMULATED	HILT	HALTINGLY	REPARATION
TRIPARTITE	MALICE	FREE SPACE	PYRE	HOARDS
SOLICITUDE	HEATHEN	HAG	WRETCHED	ASCRIBED
DISSOLUTION	BILLOWING	CHARRING	RUMINATIVE	DECREED

Beowulf Vocabulary

TRIPARTITE	NIGGARDLY	COBBLED	OMENS	TALONS
LINDEN	GROPED	HILT	UNAIDED	JACKAL
SCABBARD	BELCHING	FREE SPACE	DISSOLUTION	HOARDS
EXULTING	FURROWS	HEATHEN	PYRE	ASCRIBED
EARTHEN	RUMINATIVE	VENOM	MALICE	REPARATION

Beowulf Vocabulary

COMPELLED	CHARRING	ELUCIDATE	WRITHING	WRETCHED
SOLACE	HALTINGLY	BILLOWING	SOLICITUDE	HAG
EMULATED	RUNIC	FREE SPACE	DECREED	TARNISH
REPARATION	MALICE	VENOM	RUMINATIVE	EARTHEN
ASCRIBED	PYRE	HEATHEN	FURROWS	EXULTING

Beowulf Vocabulary

COBBLED	EXULTING	REPARATION	SOLACE	REPRISAL
NIGGARDLY	BILLOWING	EMULATED	PYRE	TRIPARTITE
WRITHING	TALONS	FREE SPACE	UNAIDED	JACKAL
DISSOLUTION	HOARDS	MALICE	CHARRING	OMENS
ELUCIDATE	COMPELLED	HILT	DECREED	RUNIC

Beowulf Vocabulary

TAUT	RUMINATIVE	ASCRIBED	LINDEN	HAG
HEATHEN	SCABBARD	FURROWS	BELCHING	TARNISH
WRETCHED	VENOM	FREE SPACE	HALTINGLY	SOLICITUDE
RUNIC	DECREED	HILT	COMPELLED	ELUCIDATE
OMENS	CHARRING	MALICE	HOARDS	DISSOLUTION